Goldfish — Silver Boot
The Story of a World War II Prisoner Of War

By Harvey S. Horn

Jacksonville, Florida ♦ Herndon, Virginia
www.Fortis-Publishing.com

Goldfish — Silver Boot
The Story of a World War II Prisoner Of War

By Harvey S. Horn

Copyright © 2010. All rights reserved. No part of this book may be reproduced or transmitted in any form or by any means, electronic or mechanical, including photocopying, recording or by any information storage and retrieval system, without written permission from the author, except for brief quotations as would be used in a review.

ISBN 978-0-9845511-9-4 (trade paperback version)

Library of Congress Control Number: 2010939178

Published by Fortis Publishing
Jacksonville, Florida—Herndon, Virginia
www.Fortis-Publishing.com

Manufactured in the United States of America

All statements of fact, opinion, or analysis expressed are those of the author and do not reflect the official positions or views of the publisher, or any U.S. Government agency or personnel. Nothing in the contents should be construed as asserting or implying U.S. Government agency or personnel's authentication of information or endorsement of the author's views. This book and subjects discussed herein are designed to provide the author's opinion in regard to the subject matter covered and is for informational purposes only.

DEDICATED TO:

The Crew of "Pretty Baby's Boys"

1st Lt. John Lincoln, Pilot

2nd Lt. Lorin Millard, Copilot

Sgt. Gilbert Caldwell, Togglier

Sgt. Edward Linnane, Flight Engineer

Sgt. Herbert Stover, Radio Operator

Cpl. Hubert Waggoner, Waist Gunner

Cpl. Oren Herrick, Waist Gunner

Cpl. Richard Michel Ball, Turret Gunner

Cpl. Louis Brown, Tail Gunner

TO ALL POWS OF ALL WARS, TO ALL VETERANS OF ALL WARS

Table of Contents

Acknowledgements	i
Foreword (about the Goldfish & Silver Boot)	iii
Introduction	1
Chapter One	3
Chapter Two	9
Chapter Three	15
Chapter Four	19
Chapter Five	21
Chapter Six	23
Chapter Seven	29
Chapter Eight	33
Chapter Nine	37
Chapter Ten	39
Pictures and Documents	**40**
Honorable Discharge Certificate	40
Crew Photo	41
In Uniform	42
In the Cockpit	43
Leroy Swindlehurst and Dan Balik	44
Fifteenth Air Force Bases	45
Central Europe Map	46
463rd Bomb Group Missions	47
Flight Record	49
Bomber Status	50
MIA Telegram	51
Letter from MG Twining	52
Letter from MG Ulio	53
Letter from MAJ Reed	54
Stalag XIII D Drawing	55
Nazi Photographs	56
Prison Camps Map	57
S.S. Prison, Torpedo Factory	58
Via Roma	59

Table of Contents (continued)

Missing Air Crew Report	60
Next of Kin List	61
Rough Map of Crash Position	62
Statement of Capture or Recovery	63
Kobylenski Statement	64
Meyerhoff Statement	65
Del Signore Statement	66
Individual Aircraft Record Card	67
Dwaine Brown Articles	68
Letter	69
Frka Email	70
NOVA Article	71
Typewritten Letter Home	72
Cablegram Home	73
BG Mollison Letter	74
Certificate of Service	75
Separation Record	76
Pass for Paris	77
Authorization for Pay	78
Travel Orders	79
Armee de L'Air	80
Appointment as Flight Officer	81
Telegram Home	82
Enlisted Record	83
Amrhein Letter	84
Lehmkuhl Letter	85
Frieda Letter	86
Photo News Article	87
Italian Photos	89
Traveler Article	91

ACKNOWLEDGEMENTS

First and foremost is my wife Minerva. Her love, guidance, support, and encouragement enabled me to write a story that was kept silent for over 55 years. Browning says, "How do I love thee. Let me count the ways." Minerva, how do I say thanks for so much?

Thanks to my great-niece Shira Ariella Wolf. She needed a story about World War II for one of her classroom assignments. It was the first time I wrote about my WW II experience.

Thanks to the Arts for Vets Program. This program is a joint venture between the Orange County Veterans Coalition and the Orange County Arts Council to offer all veterans the opportunity to explore writing, painting, rock wall construction, etc. The Orange County writers are Mary Makofske, fiction writer, poet and retired SUNY Orange English Professor; Donna Spector, playwright, fiction writer, poet and retired Vernon, NJ High School English teacher; Gretchen Gibbs, novelist and professor of Psychology at Fairleigh Dickinson University in Teaneck, NJ; Lois Karlin, former teacher and consultant who writes fiction mysteries.

I learned that good writers can paint a "picture" with a minimum of words.

Thanks to Eileen (Maggie) Fontanella, Veterans Administration volunteer and coordinator for the Library of Congress, Veterans History Project. Her patience and expertize guided me through the protocols required to record my story at the Library of Congress. It is registered under AFC/2001/001/69190.

Thanks to so many people who read my story and encouraged me to publish it. Especially, the following people, whose accomplishments in the field of literature gave me the courage to produce this book:

Dr. Anne Myles, Associate Professor, English Department, University of Northern Iowa. She read my story and thought enough of it, to give to the Head of her Department, Dr. Jeffrey Copeland.

Dr. Jeffrey A Copeland, Head of English Department, University of Northern Iowa and author of "Inman's War" and "Olivia's Story". After reading my manuscript, he said, "It's a story that must be told". He planted the seed.

Chris Godwin, Professor Emeritus, SUNY Orange. She made me a believer in "the power of story" in our lives. .

Barbara Bedell, featured columnist, Times Herald-Record, a strong supporter of all Veterans and Veterans rights. Her kind words further convinced me to publish this story.

Bob Quinn, Managing Editor of the Straus Newspapers, published my original story plus stories of my return to Foggia, Italy and to Rijecka, Croatia (Fiume, Italy). He also printed the article of my experience attending the National World War II Memorial Dedication Ceremony in Washington, DC.

FOREWORD

Allied warplanes in World War II carried out the greatest use of aircraft to reduce an enemy's ability to wage war. Never before had such devastation been inflicted on factories and cities to demoralize and destroy the enemy...

In the European Theatre of operations (ETO) American bombers bombed Axis factories and cities by day and the United Kingdom bombers bombed by night. Thousands of Allied aircraft were shot down, crashed or had to ditch in the North and Adriatic Seas.

According to Dr. Charles Stenger, formerly of the Veterans Administration with the assistance of the Department of Defense, The National Archives and the National Academy, there were 130,201 American prisoners of war. In the European Theatre of Operations (ETO), 93,941 were Army Air Corps crewmen. In the North Sea, 4,363 crewmen ditched their damaged aircraft. Only 1,538 (35%) survived. Those that survived were eligible to join the Gold Fish Club. Many more crewmen were able to escape internment or evade capture, mostly with the help of the Underground fighting the Germans.

About the Goldfish

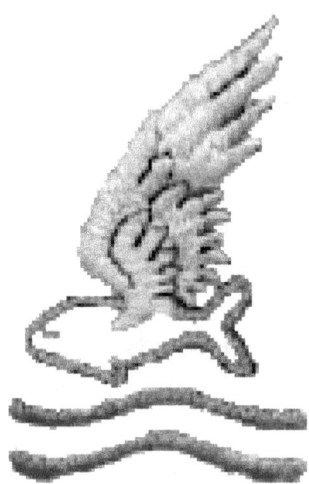

The Goldfish Club was founded in 1942 by Mr. C.A. Robertson, Chief Draughtsman of Messrs.' P.B Cow & Co. Ltd, one of the world's largest Air Sea Rescue equipment manufacturers. It was an exclusive club for airmen who had survived a wartime aircraft ditching that owed their lives to the successful use of the Mae West inflatable life preserver, rubber dinghies, or other type of life raft.

The Goldfish Club Badge shows a white-winged goldfish flying over two symbolic blue waves. The name Goldfish was selected with gold for the value of life and fish for the sea. Each new known member of the Goldfish Club was presented with a heat-sealed waterproof membership card and an embroidered badge with the financial backing of P.B. Cow. Due to wartime regulations, production of wire badges was prohibited and all cloth was severely rationed. These problems were overcome with silk embroidery substituted for wire upon black cloth cut from old evening dress suits that were sent by readers of the London Daily Express after an appeal by columnist William Hickey. Uniform dress regulations prohibited the wearing of the Goldfish Club Badge on British and American uniforms.

About the Silver Boot

SILVER BOOT INSIGNIA; this insignia was adopted by the Royal Air Forces Escaping Society founded in Paris in 1945 to help repay and show appreciation for the "HELPERS" who put their lives in danger to save downed airmen.

Many years after World War II, the mission and name was changed. In 2003, the name officially became WW2 Escape Lines Memorial Society. (ELM). There is a branch in Canada. There are several other organizations such as the Army Escape Club, Monte San Martino Trust, SOE Veterans plus Fany (former resistance workers) and MGB Crews whose members escaped or evaded capture.

The U S Air Forces Escape and Evade Society (AFEES) was founded circa, 1964. Prior to 1961, Leslie Atkinson, a captain in the French Air Force was inspired by the Royal Air Force Escape and Evade Society to form a Society of American airmen who also escaped or evaded capture by the enemy. In the spring of 1964 the Air Force Escape and Evade Society (AFEES) was officially established.

To wear these insignias, one had to survive ditching and escape from Germany during World War II.

I am honored to wear the Gold Fish and Silver Boot insignias.

INTRODUCTION

My story is about 36 days that changed my life. It is the story of a Jewish boy from Brooklyn who dreamt of flying and enlisted in the Army Air Corps to fight for his country. It is about survival. It is about walking, riding in trolleys, carts, and trains to go from Fiume, Italy to Nuremberg, Germany. It is about war. It is about the resiliency of the human being and the ability of the body to adapt to conditions beyond one's control. It is the story that all POWs keep replaying over and over and over and over. Could I have done more? Could I have done better? Did I perform as trained? Each day was a harrowing experience.

I was the navigator in John Lincoln's Crew 11-30. We were attached to the 772nd Bomber Squadron, 463rd Bomber Group, 15th Air Force based in Foggia, Italy. On March 20, 1945, we were assigned to Flying Fortress B-17G "Pretty Baby's Boys." Our mission was to bomb the marshalling yards south of Vienna at Amstettin, Austria. We were hit by flak over Zagreb, Jugoslavia, and had to ditch into Quarnaro Bay off Fiume, Italy (now Rijeka, Croatia). We became prisoners of war of the German Navy. Being captured by the Germans is not the best of times; being Jewish and being captured by the Germans is the worst of times.

The worst of times for me was to be in solitary confinement in the SS prison in Trieste, Italy, because I was Jewish. Fortunately, the Germans in northern Italy knew that the war was over for them. They honored the Geneva Convention. Earlier in the war, Jewish POWs were separated from the general Stalag population. Some were sent to concentration camps like Berga. And so, for me and John Lincoln's Crew 11-30, the journey begins. The manifest listed the crew of B-17G Flying Fortress "Pretty Baby's Boys," Serial Number 46377, as follows:

1st Lt. John Lincoln, Pilot,
29 years, Claremont, California

2nd Lt. Lorin Millard, Copilot,
26 years, Louisville, Ohio

F/O Harvey Horn, Navigator,
21 years, Brooklyn, New York

Sgt. Gilbert Caldwell, Togglier,
22 years, Modena, Utah

Sgt. Edward Linnane, Flight Engineer,
25 years, Chicago, Illinois

Sgt. Herbert Stover, Radio Operator,
19 years, Philadelphia, Pennsylvania

Cpl. Hubert Waggoner, Waist Gunner,
20, years, Hillsboro, Illinois

Cpl. Oren Herrick, Waist Gunner,
20 years, Cleveland, Ohio

Cpl. Richard Michel Ball, Turret Gunner,
24 years Stamph, Arkansas

Cpl. Louis Brown, Tail Gunner,
18 years, Hillsboro, Illinois

CHAPTER ONE

I grew up listening to the radio heroes like the Green Hornet, the Shadow, Agent X9, and many others. The moving pictures gave us heroes who wore white hats. The FBI and the military were beyond reproach. It was my country, right or wrong. I read all the Zane Grey books, Henry David Thoreau, Mark Twain, Popular Mechanics and especially the magazines about World War I Flying Aces. My friends and I built model airplanes out of balsa wood, paper and cement. We never thought about sniffing the cement. Most of the planes I built were from kits. Some were from my own designs. I used to hang the models on a string and run them across the ceiling of my bedroom. It drove my mother wild. She couldn't take the glue cement smell. On the Fourth of July, my friends and I would go to the roofs of our houses, load the models up with firecrackers, light them up and let them fly.

On December 7, 1941, I was listening to the New York Giants football game on the radio. At about 4:00 p.m., the program was interrupted with a news flash: The Japanese bombed Pearl Harbor. I rushed into the kitchen to tell my parents and ask, "Where is Pearl Harbor?" The next day, President Roosevelt declared war on Japan. Then Germany and Italy, who were the Axis partners of Japan, declared war on us. Of course, I was aware of the war in Europe, but like many seventeen-year-old teenagers, it didn't really have an impact on me.

Upon graduating from Erasmus Hall High School, I enrolled at Pratt Institute, School of Engineering to study Mechanical Engineering. After two semesters at Pratt, I decided to enlist in the Army Air Corps. On October 30, 1942, without my parent's knowledge or consent, I took the subway to the Manhattan Recruiting Center at 70 Church Street to enlist in the Army Air Corps. I passed both the physical and written aptitude tests. Only half of those that had applied that day passed the physical test. Half of those remaining failed the written test. I was going to be an Army Air Corps cadet.

I rushed out of the recruiting center to find the closest phone to call my folks. I spotted a phone booth on the other side of Church Street. Without looking in either direction for oncoming cars, I ran across the double lane street. My career in the Air Corps would have ended there, except for the quick reaction of a Ford convertible driver with a K in the license plate

"Whatsamattawitchuse? You gotta look you know!"

I knew he was from Brooklyn without seeing the K on the license plate.

I dug into my pocket and found a nickel. Placing the coin into the slot, my heart beat a steady thump, thump, thump. I dialed my house. It rang once, twice, three times. Where are they? Finally, my mother picked up.

"Mom, Mom, I made it! I was accepted in the Army Air Corps Cadet program!" I went on, "Only twenty five percent were accepted!" On the other end of the phone, there was complete silence. "Mom? Are you there?" Finally, my mother's voice very quietly said, "Yes, I'm here." I didn't realize then what a shock it was for her to learn that her only son had enlisted and was going to war. As a college student, I probably could have been deferred for many months. As it turned out, it took almost six months and I was able to complete another semester before I was called up.

In early February, I received a letter from the Army Air Corps to report for basic training on March 18, 1943, at Atlantic City, New Jersey. On the morning of March 18, my mother packed a small valise with personal items: a toothbrush, underwear, etc. We took the BMT subway to the Pennsylvania Train Station on Eighth Avenue and 33rd Street in Manhattan. The station was abuzz with soldiers and civilians crisscrossing the station to get to their gates. We had to sidestep a group led by Bob Hope leading his USO entourage like the wedge at an Oldtimers football game. We arrived at the gate marked Atlantic City. It was a tearful bon voyage. We hugged and kissed. I promised to write, maybe not often but I would write. I can only imagine, what they said to each other as they took the subway home. I remember my thoughts were only on what I would find in Atlantic City. I was picturing myself as the flyboy in those World War I magazine stories.

Home was the Traymore Hotel. In its glory days, it was one of the premier hotels on the Boardwalk. It was still very impressive. The rooms had high ceilings and were large enough to bed four cadets. The lobby was styled in Art Deco. I tried to imagine how it looked before the war with soft, deep couches and coffee tables. Now, with hundreds of cadets milling about, there was little furniture to be found. After thirty days of drills, walking the Boardwalk to the music of Glenn Miller, calisthenics at the Convention Center, manuals on Army rules and regulations, we were ready for pre-preflight training. We would be given ten hours of instruction in piloting the single engine Piper Cub airplane.

After a ten-hour train ride, our group arrived at the University of Vermont in Burlington. It was within shouting distance of the Canadian border on Lake Champlain. Of course, you had to shout real loud. The Army Air Corps had contracted with a number of colleges and universities to train cadets prior to classification. After weeks of strenuous calisthenics and many hours of studying aerodynamics, mechanics and airport runway procedures, we were finally ready to take the controls of the Piper Cubs. The vision of me in a cockpit, ala the World War I aces, was coming true, except for one thing: I would be flying a single high wing 75-horse powered Wright engine aircraft. I learned to do spins, figure eights around barns and haystacks, and to recover from stalls. It was the best of both worlds: college campus life and flying.

In mid-June, we "graduated." We took another 14-hour train ride to Nashville, Tennessee, for classification. Nashville is not a great place to be in June. The weather was very hot and humid. I was put through another battery of aptitude tests. We were asked to list our choices: pilot, navigator or bombardier. I qualified for all three. Of course, I chose pilot.

I looked forward to primary flight training. I dreamt about flying the PT-17 Stearman biplane, flying helmet on my head, goggles over my eyes, white satin scarf around my neck, slightly tucked in my A4 leather jacket, just like the World War I aces. I was sent to Maxwell Field, Montgomery, Alabama, for preflight training. If you think Nashville in June is hot, try Montgomery, Alabama in July. The next three months we spent studying flight dynamics, radio and Morse code. We endured grueling calisthenics, 10-mile cross country runs, and the Burma Road obstacle course. Little did I know that this conditioning would help me survive internment as a prisoner of war.

Primary training was a short train ride to Orangeburg, South Carolina. Sadly, I "washed out." At nineteen, I was not able to master the controls in the time allotted. I felt a little better when I learned that a cadet who had flown as a test pilot in civilian life also washed out. The Air Corps needed pilots as quickly as they could be trained. I was given my second choice, navigation. I was a very sad and dejected cadet as I waited for the train to take me to Fort Myers, Florida. My dream of being a pilot ended.

All navigators and bombardiers had to be qualified gunners. I earned my "Gunnery Wings" at Fort Myers, Florida. I was bussed from Fort Myers via the Okeechobee Trail to the Pan American Airways school of Navigation at Dinner Key, Florida. Home was the San Sebastian Hotel in Coral Gables, Florida. Classes and physical training were conducted at

Miami University, otherwise known as the West Point of the South. We followed the same regimen as the cadets at West Point: honor code; hazing by upperclassmen; white glove inspections; square meals; double time everywhere we went. Demerits resulted in walking a "tour" in full dress, white gloves and a carbine on the shoulder.

Pan American was a contract school that taught primarily celestial navigation. I had to memorize 64 major stars. Navigation flight training was conducted in the famous two engine Consolidated Commodore Clipper Flying Boats (top speed of 85 knots per hour). In the thirties, these planes flew to Central and South America. We trained by plotting simulated flights in addition to actual day and night flights. The simulated flights consisted of many legs. We were given the take off point, destinations, air speed, weather conditions and altitude. We had to plot the course to arrive at the destination. You were graded on time and distance to touch down. The top score was zero, zero.

Seasoned Pan American pilots flew the Sikorsky and the Consolidated Commodore aircraft. Taking off in a flying boat is much different than on land. The pilot would pull full power to get the hull moving like a speedboat. It was called getting on the "step." At speeds of 75-knots, the pilot would yo yo the yoke to bounce the hull out of the water. This technique was used to break the meniscus. A take off run of several miles was common.

Landing on water requires more skill than on land. The pilot has to watch carefully the altimeter and air speed because depth perception is more difficult to read over water, more so when landing at night. One night we were returning from a training flight when the pilot started to descend in a slow glide. Looking out of the side window, I could see that the approach was too steep. Just as I started to say "Pull up, Pull up" I heard a loud thud and saw through the window what looked like a small boat off to the side. My God! Did we hit a fisherman? On closer look, it was our right pontoon. We had groundlooped in the Bay. Fortunately, the wing did not hit the water or we would have plunged into the bay. The next day, Pan Am conducted an inquiry. All the cadets on this flight gave depositions. Later, we found out that the Captain of the plane was demoted. He was a seasoned pilot with 15,000 flying hours.

On August 26, 1944, I was honorably discharged from the Army Air Corps and "reenlisted" in order to receive my Navigation Wings as Flight Officer Harvey Horn. The Air Corps had to create a new designation because they had too many lieutenants. Flight officers had the rank and privileges of a lieutenant, but they were not "commissioned" - only the ten per cent were commissioned.

CHAPTER TWO

In early September, I reported to Drew Field, Tampa, Florida, after a short leave to visit my family in Brooklyn, New York. Drew and McDill Fields were Army Air Corps bases where crews trained as a unit before heading overseas. I was assigned to Crew 11-30 as Navigator on a B17 Flying Fortress. I was 19 years old. I was the youngest officer in the crew, although at the time I didn't realize that I was seven to ten years younger than the other officers. The crew came from all parts of the country.

The Crew 11-30 consisted as follows:

    1st Lt. John Lincoln, Pilot
    29 years Claremont, California

    2nd Lt. Lorin Millard, Copilot
    26 years Louisville, Ohio

    2nd Lt. George Kall Bombardier
    26 years Rochester, New York

    Sgt. Edward Linnane Flight Engineer
    25 years Chicago, Illinois

    Sgt. Herbert Stover Radio Operator
    19 years Philadelphia, Pennsylvania

    Cpl. Hubert Waggoner Waist Gunner
    20 years Hillsboro, Indiana

    Cpl. Oren Herrick Waist Gunner
    20 years Cleveland, Ohio

    Cpl. Richard Michel Ball Turret Gunner
    24 years Stamph, Arkansas

    Cpl. Louis Brown Tail Gunner
    18 years Hillsboro, Illinois

Flight training off the Florida Gulf Coast was routine. We flew almost every day to become familiar with each other and the techniques of flying in bomber formations. One day we were called to take a VIP to Maxwell Field, Montgomery, Alabama. The officers had all gone through classification at Maxwell. It was like going back to one's elementary school. As I walked from the hangar to the administration house, passing cadets saluted. I smiled as I remembered when I had to salute all officers.

The flight from Maxwell back to Tampa was a nightmare. The weather had turned ugly. Cumulus nimbus clouds (otherwise known as CBs) were building up. I gave John and Lorin the headings to Drew. About an hour into the flight, the magnetic compass started bouncing. Cloud coverage precluded dead reckoning by sighting landmarks. Celestial shots were impossible. The radio was cracking up with severe static. I could not get another bearing. John and I tried the airline radio directional. Nothing. Frankly, I was lost. I tried retracing the heading and air speed. I decided to use a four square method. Fly for 5 minutes on one heading, then 90-degrees for another five minutes, another 90-degree turn for five. Somehow, we were able to pick up a signal from Atlanta Airport. I knew about where we were. After arriving back at Drew, I checked with the other navigators that had been in the air. They, too, had all been lost.

After several months of training, our crew was assigned to the European Theatre of Operations (ETO). On January 24, 1945, we took the train to Savannah, Georgia, and picked up a new B-17G Flying Fortress at Hunter Field. For the next two weeks we worked to make the plane combat ready. I calibrated all the instruments. The gunners checked their 50-caliber machine guns. George, our bombardier, checked the Norden bombsight.

One day John took us up for an altitude test flight. I got to sit in the copilot seat and fly the B-17. I did a lot better than my experience with the Stearman PT-17. John decided to see how high this baby could fly. Up, up and away. 30,000, 32,000 34,000; we were still climbing. At 38,200 feet the Boeing B-17G started to groan and moan. That was it. John peeled off like he was a fighter pilot on a strafing mission. We got down a lot faster than we went up.

Finally, we were given sealed orders to fly overseas. After we leveled off to our cruising altitude, John opened the sealed orders. We were assigned to the 15th Air Force, 463rd Bomber Group, 772nd Bomber Squadron, based in Foggia, Italy. I laid out the flight plan that would take us from Savannah to Bari, Italy, stopping at Elmira, New York, Gander, Newfoundland, the Azores and Marrakech, Morocco.

We landed at the Elmira airport in a severe snowstorm. Ed Linnane found gloves for us to wear to cover the engines with tarps. The weather cleared the next morning and we took off for Gander. Flying over the Northeast into Canada was a kaleidoscope of browns, whites, greens plus a mixture of the other colors in the rainbow. Sitting in the nose of a B-17 Flying Fortress, cruising at 10,000 feet, is like licking an ice cream cone at a baseball game. You want both the ice cream and the game to last.

We arrived at Gander as the sun was setting. In the winter, Gander, Newfoundland, is very, very cold and windy. Again, the gloves were put on and the engines covered. We had planned to depart at 6:00 p.m. for the Azores, but hydraulic repairs delayed our departure until 1:00 a.m. Taking off the tarps in a howling wind with temperatures below zero is an exhausting job. Everything is stiff and frozen. Takeoff was routine. As we climbed to our cruising altitude of 12,000 feet, the overcast cleared and every star in the galaxy came out to greet us. I would remember this sight forever. One nice thing about flying over water is that pilots will follow your headings to a tee.

I spent the next hours taking readings on Vega, Altair and Deneb, three of the brightest stars in the northern sky. I gave John the compass headings and the ETA (Estimated Time of Arrival) of 9:30 GMT. It was a quiet flight. The crew slept while John, Lorin and I watched the store. Dawn was breaking. I was fascinated by the sun rising directly in front of the nose of the plane. I gave John another heading correction and time to start our descent into Sao Miguel Island, Azores. I hit the Azores, zero, zero. On target and on time.

It is a beautiful island. I was able to walk into town and shop the stores. The craftsmanship of the filigree silver pins and pendants was outstanding. I regretted that I didn't buy some souvenirs. We left the Azores the next morning for Morocco. Arriving in Marrakesh about noontime, the temperature was over 100 degrees with eighty per cent humidity. Again, we covered the engines: this time to prevent the dry dust from clogging the intake lines. There was no need for the gloves. John, Lorin and George went into city to the Grand Bazaar. They brought back bottles of gin. My exposure to hard liquor was to sip my father's Teacher's scotch on rare occasions and a glass of wine at the Seder table on Passover. I became deathly sick. It was many, many years before I would drink gin again.

The flight from Marrakesh to Bari took us over the city of Oran, crossing the Mediterranean Sea, along the sole and heel of Italy's boot and up the east coast. We landed at Bari and turned the B-17 over to the 15th Air Force. Trucks took us to Foggia. Foggia was the most heavily bombed city in Italy; first by the Germans and then by the U.S. Air Force. I remember stopping at an intersection in Foggia because of a noisy crowd blocking the road. A GI had been cut on his face by an irate Italian. The GI had apparently been fooling around with the Italian's wife. Welcome to Foggia, Italy.

We arrived at the Celoni Air Field at about twenty-one hours. The airfield was five miles northwest of Foggia. John, Lorin, George and I were assigned to a tent with Squadron Navigator 1st Lt. Leroy (Roy) Swindlehurst. (Many years later, I would meet his son Joel, who became the historian of the 463rd Bomber Group organization.) Wooden buildings housed the Officers Club, Mess Hall and Operations, latrines and showers. There were open areas for sports activities. Food was good. We had powdered eggs for breakfast. Crews scheduled to fly a combat mission would have real eggs. Each day we practiced dry runs with the 772nd Squadron. We flew both as a crew and with other crews to gain experience. The 463rd Bomber Group was part of the 5th Wing of the 15th Air Force that flew B17s. All the other Bomber Groups flew B24s. There were sayings/superstitions: "You flew in the same underwear (longjohns)" and "A crew that stayed together would go home together". The list goes on. Celoni Air Field had a quonset hut at the beginning of the runway. That was my landmark. Whenever I saw that, I knew I was home.

Navigators not assigned to fly a mission, plotted the next day's mission. I would go to the Operations building at about 3:00 a.m., when Group Headquarters received the latest intelligence and weather conditions. The Americans flew day missions. The Aussies and New Zealanders flew night missions in British Wellingtons. Occasionally I would go down to the runway to watch them take off.

On March 14, 1945, the next day's mission was posted. Herb Stover and I were assigned to fly with another crew. As I read my name on the post up sheet, I felt my heart skip a beat. This was it. My first mission. All the many months of training were over. This was the payoff. This is why I enlisted in the Air Corps. I was finally going to bomb the enemy. Surprisingly, I felt no anxiety.

I awoke at 4:30 a.m. and dressed in the dark for the mission. It was March 15, 1945. I took special care not to wake John, Lorin, George and Roy. Outside of the tent, it was dark, cold and windy. I followed several of the other crews that were assigned to fly to the mess tent. I got my first taste of real eggs since arriving in Italy.

After breakfast, I picked up my navigation gear and went to the briefing room, a low wooden building adjacent to the Operations building. The room had chairs arranged in rows with a wide aisle down the middle. In the front of the room was a raised platform. Above the platform was a large map that was covered with a bed sheet and overhead lamps. The small windows on each side of the building were also covered with dark drapes. Herb Stover and I sat together. We would be flying with a seasoned crew. The room was buzzing with chatter, crews ribbing each other. The air was filled with cigarette smoke. There was a mixture of anxious laughs and serenity in the room as we waited for the Group Commander to brief us on the mission. The Sergeant at the door shouted to bring us to attention. We scrambled to our feet as the Group Commander came in followed by the weatherman and intelligence people.

The mission was Ruhrland, Germany, 75 miles south of Berlin. Our target was the marshalling yards. This would normally be an 8th Air Force target but bad weather over England kept their Bombers grounded. It would become the longest mission ever flown by the 15th Air Force. The bed sheet was removed and a large map showed our flight plan. Black circles marked locations of heavy anti-aircraft locations; German fighter groups were marked with red circles. Next came the meteorology report: winds, cloud coverage, altitude. Maps were distributed to the navigators. Flight leaders were briefed on the bombing run (initial point to target). We would be escorted to the target by P-38 Lightnings and picked up by P-47 Thunderbolts on our return leg.

It was still dark as we made our way to the flight line. Pilots and flight engineers did a 360-degree walk through checking our B-17. Once inside, the pilot and copilot started the flight check. The bombardier checked the Norden bombsight. I checked my maps and weather data. I mentally noted options to change course should fighter or anti-aircraft damage our B-17. At 6:30 GMT, with the sun starting to rise, a flare went off signaling the pilots to start their engines. Shortly, a second flare was shot. Slowly, the lead B-17 left the parking slot and taxied to the runway. Flaps down, full power, release brakes. The heavy B-17 loaded with 2000 pounds of bombs lumbered down the runway. At 20-second intervals, the other B-17s followed their leader.

At about 8,000 feet, our B-17 burst through the light morning fog. I could see B-17s popping up through the mist and start to circle to form up in squadrons and groups. All I could think of was they looked like rabbits heads popping out of their holes. Just before we tightened the flying formation, the pilot ordered the gunners to check their 50-caliber guns by firing a few short bursts. This was standard practice. We started to gain altitude as we crossed the Adriatic Sea. The P-38 fighter planes came into view. What a sight, their silver wings glistening. I could see the pilots' faces as they gave us the thumbs up sign. They took positions, high and low. By the time we crossed over the Italian Alps into Austria, we had attained our cruising altitude of 28,500 feet.

As we approached the heartland of Germany, the anti-aircraft batteries opened up on us. I could see the four puffs of flak exploding above and behind the Group. The odds of being hit were very low when the puffs were random shots. However, when the batteries found your altitude and speed, it was only a matter of time before you were hit. The flak got real heavy as we approached the IP (Inital Point). I could hear the ping as it went through the thin aluminum skin. The pilot released the controls of the B-17 to the Bombardier. He would use the automatic pilot attached to the Norden bombsight to guide the plane over the target. He hunched down over the sight. I checked my flak jacket to be sure it gave me the maximum coverage. I took my position directly behind him with my chest against his back. I felt connected to him like there was an invisible bond between us. I concentrated on his procedures. The entire crew would be at the mercy of the 88mm anti-aircraft batteries for the next ten minutes until the bombs dropped. Just as the bombs dropped, I heard another ping and saw the bombardier's upper left arm jump. He had been hit with flak. I quickly cut open his flight jacket and applied sulphur to the wound. It was not deep and didn't appear to have broken any bones. I still shudder when I think back that if the flak missed his arm, it would have hit me in the head. The other crewmembers were reporting hits but no casualties.

The pilot banked sharply to the left and headed for home. Our fighter coverage cleared the skies of enemy fighter planes. We had an uneventful flight home. There was very little fuel in the tanks as I saw the Quonset structure. We were home. The bombardier was taken to the hospital. I walked around our ship. It was riddled with flak holes. I was not sure if this plane would ever fly again. Many of the B-17's in the Group had to land in Jugoslavia on emergency fields. It was a successful mission.

It would be 5 days before I was to fly my second mission.

CHAPTER THREE

March 20, 1945, was a clear sunny day. It would be the day that forever changed my life. I would no longer be the boy that built balsa wood planes, played punch ball in the streets of Brooklyn, believed in my country right or wrong, and the FBI. I dreamt of flying in a Spad Biplane, a silk scarf wrapped around my neck, goggles over my eyes, ala a World War I Ace.

Approaching Zagreb, Jugoslavia, at 30,000 feet, I was sitting in the nose of my B-17 Flying Fortress "Pretty Baby's Boys." I was mesmerized by the wispy white entrails that floated from the four Pratt & Whitney engines. Everywhere I looked, there were Flying Fortresses in V formations, their engines cutting through the thin air. We were in the number four slot of Bomber Squadron, 772nd, E Group. Our mission was to bomb the marshalling yards south of Vienna in Amstettin, Austria.

This was our first mission as Crew 11-30. Except for copilot 2nd Lt. Lorin Millard, we had been on other missions to gain experience with seasoned crews. In front of me was Gilbert Caldwell, togglier. He was substituting for Lt. George Kall, our crew bombardier. The nose of a B-17 was not designed for fat or tall men. The Plexiglas front had two ports for the 50-caliber machine gun. I had the left side. Gil covered the right side, should "bandits" attack. I could touch the aluminum walls of the bomber by extending my arms and had to bend my neck slightly to stand. I crouched over the navigation desk checking location and time to IP and position of the 88mm anti-aircraft guns. Gil was checking the Norden bombsight.

The temperature at 30,000 feet is minus 60 degree F. I wore a heated felt undersuit and slippers, olive drab shirt and pants, a fur lined olive drab jacket with the yellow Mae West resting on my shoulders. The heated suits and slippers were less bulky than the old leather fleece lined flying suits. My GI shoes were dangling from the parachute harness strapped to my chest. A Government issue Colt .45 sidearm hung from my hip. The oxygen mask was securely locked over my mouth and nose. When we reached enemy territory, the heavy flak vest would drape over my shoulders. Gil was similarly dressed. We looked like men from Mars.

Today the Bomber Group would be pattern bombing. When the lead bombardier drops his bomb load, the other bombers drop their bombs. Our bombing run (from initial point to target) was 11 minutes. For 11 minutes, we would be a target for the anti-aircraft gunners to lock in on our speed and altitude. It was like we were the sitting ducks at a shooting gallery.

Flak is what we call the shells fired by the anti- aircraft guns. It is pressure set to explode at a given altitude into four puffs of black smoke and fragments. If the four puffs exploded randomly (high, low, in front or in back of the plane), the odds were in our favor of not being hit. If the puffs were coming in at our altitude, it was only a matter of time before we would be hit. Eleven minutes over Vienna was a real sweat job.

Suddenly, the steady drone of those powerful engines was broken by intercom shouts from the tail gunner Brownie. Then Radio Operator Herb Stover broke in: "Flak at 6 o'clock!" "Pretty Baby's Boys" shuddered as Number 3 engine sputtered and died. In rapid succession, like a 50-caliber machine gun spurt, John started to issue orders:

"Lorin, feather the number three, it's spinning out of control."

"Damage report!"

"Anyone hit?"

"Harv, where the hell are we?"

"How far to the coast?"

"Call E Group leader."

"We're losing altitude."

"Ed, check the hydraulic system."

"Prepare to bail out!"

I checked the maps and time. My chronometer read 14:48 GMT (2:48 p.m.). We were about 60 miles from the coast. Could we make it over the Jugoslavian Alps? A quick decision was made. "Let's go for it!" John barked into the intercom. "Hold it, we are going to try for the coast." No answer. The intercom was dead. Lorin went back to the galleyway to stop the crew from bailing out. Oren Herrick was at the door ready to jump. A B-17 can fly on three engines, maybe even two engines. I gave John the heading. E Group Commander, 1st Lt. Thaddeus Kosylesky concurred that our best shot was to make it to the coast where there were emergency landing strips. John passed the word: Jettison everything that isn't bolted down.

The Number 2 engine sputtered and died. Oil was leaking from Number 1. We were losing altitude more rapidly. Everything went out: flak vests, 50-caliber machine guns, ammunition, books, and personal gear - including the parachute harnesses with our GI shoes. Only Lorin kept his shoes. The guys even tried to unbolt the lower ball turret. I picked what looked like open farmland and instructed Gill to drop our bomb load. We were committed. We were going to make it or crash into the Alps. It would be the longest 20 minutes of my young life.

Flying on two engines, I could almost touch the snow-covered peaks as our B-17 cleared the Alps. The reflection from the sun on the snow was blinding. All eyes were on the alert for German fighter planes. All clear. We had the nose, top, tail and ball turret machine guns still combat ready. We kept losing altitude. The Number 1 engine started to sputter. Smoke and fire was coming out of the cowling. We could see the city of Fiume, Italy (now Rijeka, Croatia), below the horizon. Any hope of getting to the emergency fields was lost. It was a race to get to the sea and ditch "Pretty Baby's Boys" or crash into the rugged Croatian mountains that surrounded Fiume. With extraordinary skill, John and Lorin were able to keep the plane level as we passed over the city at 500 feet. Anti-aircraft batteries strategically placed around the city opened fire. The flak cut through the aluminum body creating an anvil chorus.

We took our ditch positions. We had practiced this procedure back in the states, never envisioning that we would actually put it to use. We followed the procedures quietly, confidently, quickly taking the designated positions. There was no hysteria or fear. All hatches were opened. Smokey Stover inflated his Mae West and positioned himself at the radio desk. Waggoner, Michael, Brownie and I sat facing the rear of the plane with our backs against the bulkhead. The other three sat against the other bulkhead facing us. We hit the waters of Quarnaro Bay at 100 miles per hour. First, the tail hit with a terrific jolt, then the ball turret, jerking the nose downward slowing the bomber down. This was followed by a series of jolts, tail, nose, tail, nose that I felt with every bone in my body. "Pretty Baby's Boys" settled into the shark infested waters of Quarnaro Bay, part of the Adriatic Sea.* Twenty and a half minutes had elapsed from the time we were first hit by flak to ditching our aircraft into Quarnaro Bay.** The seawater gushed in from all sides. Barely able to see, we scrambled up the escape ladder. Some of the crew waded to the waist gunner ports and swam to the wings. John and Lorin escaped through the cockpit windows that were blown out, the rubber dinghies were released from the compartments just behind the pilot and copilot's seats. The one on the left side inflated automatically. The one on the right side had to be hand inflated. We slid down the wings and crawled into the rubber boats, five men in each. I took one of the oars and started to paddle toward a distant island. The bay was fairly calm. As I pressed my body forward to get better leverage to drive the heavy rubber boat forward, I caught the bright reflection of the sun from the tail of "Pretty Baby's Boys." I watched the water slowly cover the upper fuselage, then the nose and finally the tail. Flying Fortress B-17G-50, Serial Number 44-6377, born July 18, 1944, at Douglas, Long Beach, California, named "Pretty Baby's Boys," died March 20, 1945, on its fourth mission. I said it took about eight minutes for it to sink. Lorin thought it was longer. It rests at the bottom of Quarnaro Bay. "Yisgadall vei Yisgadash." An old Hebrew prayer for the departed.

The water was cold but not freezing. The sun started to dry out our water logged flying suits. Within minutes, we could see a large boat leaving the docks of Fiume, heading toward us. The German gunboat pulled alongside. German sailors pointed their machine guns at us and motioned for us to drop our Colt .45 side arms. Lines were attached to the front of each dinghy and slowly we were towed the six miles to the wharves of Fiume. We had survived the flak over Zagreb and ditching off Fiume. Lou Brown was hit by flak in the right hand. John had a cut over his nose when his head hit the yoke. (He did not inflate his Mae West as we hit the water.) I learned after 60 years that I had sustained a broken toe. We were bruised, bleeding, wet, tired and hungry, but we were alive. We were now MIAs and POWs.

*Twelve year old Ivo Simonic was sitting on a hill with friends and heard the roar of the B-17 engine. On the other side of the city, twelve-year-old Stelio Vranich also heard the same roar. They both looked up and saw our B17 heading to the water, two engines dead, one on fire with smoke trailing and only one engine turning over. Ivo remembered seeing two SS German Officers watching us through their binoculars. He heard one say to the other, "The pilot must be very efficient and competent."

** Lou Brown's watch shattered when we hit the water. It read 15:04:1/2 GMT (3:04:1/2)

CHAPTER FOUR

The German Wehrmacht took over from the Navy and formed a semi-circle around us. They ordered us to march toward a wide street that led up a small hill to the center of the city. The people of Fiume lined the street of Via Roma to see the "circus" that came to town. Except, we were the animals. Most just stared at us. A few made hostile remarks. The 15th Air Force had bombed this city many, many times.***

We continued up the cobblestone street, passed by St. Vitas Church to a large manor like house with high wooden gates. Upon entering, we were lined up in the courtyard against a large wall, pockmarked from machine gun and shellfire. The German soldiers stood in front of each of us, their machine guns pointing at us. I was sure they were going to shoot us. We stood there for what seem like an eternity but was probably 10 minutes.

A Sergeant motioned to us to follow him into the manor. We entered the first floor that had a very large room with wooden tables, benches and chairs. At the far end were doors that presumably led to small offices. Each one of us was stripped and searched. One by one, we were led into a room for interrogation. A German Officer asked for our name, organization and mission. We gave our name, rank and serial number in accordance with the Geneva Convention.

When we reassembled in the large room, we all looked at each other. We all had the same thought: They were going to shoot us as we stood with our backs against the grey wall. Shortly, they brought out black bread and ersatz coffee. It tasted like wine and cake. I hadn't eaten since breakfast about 6:00 a.m.

Night had fallen. I laid down on my back on one of the wooden benches. I could see the stars through the small high windows. I clutched my dog tag with the H for Hebrew embossed on it. Dog tags carried the religious affiliation of the individual soldiers. P stood for Protestant, C for Catholic and H for Hebrew. I was a Jew in the hands of the Germans. For the first time, I started to think of what would happen to me. I never, ever, ever, thought about being captured by the Germans. It just never entered my mind. Exhausted, I dozed off.

*** The 15th Air Force had repeatedly bombed a torpedo factory in Fiume. The torpedo was invented here by Giovanni Luppisin in 1866. It was perfected by an English engineer named Whitehead.

CHAPTER FIVE

The sunlight shining through the small high windows woke me up. Every bone in my body ached. I don't know whether it was from the pummeling my body took when we ditched or sleeping on the hard bench. Probably, it was a little of both. I thought of my GI boots lost somewhere in Jugoslavia. German soldiers armed with machine guns came in and motioned for us to follow them into another room where we were given black bread and hot tea. After using the toilets, we marched out into the courtyard with an ominous high grey wall. I will never forget that grey wall.

A new group of German soldiers came out of a door on the far side of the courtyard. They appeared to be in their thirties, and would be our guards. We marched up a short hill to a trolley station. It was the morning "rush" hour. Very few Italians paid any attention to us. We boarded the trolley that would take us to Trieste. It was crowded, no different from the subways in New York City during rush hour. No attempt was made to segregate us. We stood shoulder to shoulder with our guards and the Italians. I remember looking, no staring, at a beautiful young dark haired Italian girl. The angle of the sun silhouetted her bosom through the thin cotton blouse. She was not wearing a bra. Even in my perilous situation, I continued to stare. She gave no sign that she knew I was there.

After an hour, we arrived in Trieste. Trieste is a very old city that once was a major commercial center. There were signs of rubble and destruction in the streets from American bombing raids. As we walked through the streets protected by our guards, the citizens glared at us. We came to an old grey four-storey building where the German SS held Italian partisans and political prisoners. John, Lorin, Ed Linnane and I were put into a five foot by five-foot cell. The others were divided into small groups and placed in similar cells. The menu was consistent. Twice a day, we were given black bread, ersatz coffee or tea and cabbage/onion soup served in tin coffee cans. It was hot water with strands of cabbage or onions. It tasted like my mother's chicken soup

The floor was covered with a layer of straw. It didn't take long for the lice to make their home in our armpits and hair. There was a small two foot wide by three foot wide iron barred window, about six feet high, facing a U shaped courtyard. I could see the third and fourth floors of the prison where Italian partisans were held. News of our capture passed through the prison like wildfire. The German guards told us how much the partisans appreciated the Americans.

The next morning we were taken one by one into another section of the prison to be interrogated. John went first. He was gone about two hours. When he returned, Lorin was taken out. John said he gave name, rank and serial number. He also said that the Germans knew a great deal about each of us: when we had arrived in Foggia, the 463rd Bomber Group, 772nd Bomber Squadron, "Pretty Baby's Boys," and so on. Primarily, they wanted confirmations.

After a few hours, Lorin returned and I was taken to interrogation. Except, I was taken to another section of the prison and placed into a small dark closet. The closet was about three feet by eight feet with no windows. When my eyes adjusted, I could see the door and the ceiling. I ran my hands over all the surfaces to see if there were any knobs or recesses that I could open. No such luck. It was the worst day of my life. I went to one far corner and relieved myself. Then, I lay down as far away from there as I could. I started to shiver uncontrollably. I wrapped my arms about my chest and tried to relax to keep warm. I thought of my mother and father. They will never know what happened to me. I clutched my dog tag with the H embossed on it. When I enlisted, I never, ever thought about the possibility of my being captured, much less, by the Germans. It just never crossed my mind. I don't know how long I lay there going over and over who I was, what I was. Finally, after much agonizing, I made a decision: I am Jewish. I will always be Jewish. Fuck 'em. Even though they must know I'm Jewish from my dog tags, I will tell them. A huge load was lifted from my chest. I relaxed and started to fall asleep. I started thinking about growing up in the Borough Park section of Brooklyn, my enlisting in Army Air Corps and my journey to Trieste.

CHAPTER SIX

I had no idea how long I was held in the closet. Though I had stopped shivering, I was still chilled to the bone. I got up and did double time in place to get the circulation going. The closet was too confined to walk. Hunger pangs started to come. As I tried to doze off I thought about how my family would receive the news I was "Missing in Action." The smell from relieving myself was making the closet pungent. Finally, I heard a slight noise at the door. The door creaked open. By squinting, I could see two guards. I stumbled through the doorway. They motioned to me to follow them down a long hallway that led to a highly polished door with brass knobs and German lettering. One knock, "Arouse!" The door opened and sitting behind a large desk was a blonde Aryan looking German. He was about thirty with the shoulder insignia of a Captain. His uniform was pressed. I did not see any SS markings. I stood there for several minutes as he looked over some papers from a folder. He finally looked up and motioned for me to sit down in the chair opposite him. The guards left. I remained facing him for several minutes as he continued to study the folder.

In a pleasant, calm, quiet voice, he started to question me. He told me that the others had given him information about our airfield, bomber group and, bomber squadron. My reply was name, rank and serial number. He talked; I listened. This went on for several minutes He continued talking about our base in Foggia. Finally, we got to the dreaded subject of the H on my dog tag. Yes, I am Jewish.

He went into a long story, much of it I don't remember. He said, essentially, American Jews were different from European Jews. I am not sure how long the interrogation lasted. When I was finally returned to the cell, John, Lorin and Ed just nodded at me but didn't ask what had happened. Years later Lorin told me that they thought I was put into solitary because I was Jewish. I think that I survived because the Germans in Italy knew that the war was lost. I was very fortunate. The Germans separated Jewish servicemen from other POWs in the Stalags. Some, like my friend Gerry Daub, were sent to the Berga concentration camp.

We remained in the cramped cell for five days. I can't remember exactly how I passed the time. Lorin remembers going on a garbage detail. I have no such memory. What I do remember is curling up on the floor, gripping my knees, waiting for food, the grey prison walls, the bars, the third and fourth levels, onion soup, black bread, and ersatz coffee that made you run to the toilet. Picking lice from my underarms became a sport. More painful, however, is my recollection of the high-pitched sounds of the partisans and political prisoners who suffered under horrible conditions. I was told that some of the partisans were hung with meat hooks through their jaws. Fortunately, the high windows prevented me from seeing this atrocity.

On the morning of the sixth day, we were taken through the same wooden doors where we had entered. Trucks were waiting to take us to the train station for the ride to the Basaldella Camp outside of Udine, Italy. The camp consisted of many two-storey wooden barracks. Accommodations were better than in Trieste. We had cots in one large room and the mess consisted of potato soup served in bowls and the usual black bread and ersatz coffee. The Germans guarded the front and back doors. Sgt. Hasselmann was in charge of the detail. One day, we were coming back from the mess hall when a B-24 Liberator came in low over the barracks. The German anti-aircraft 88mm guns opened fire on them. Flak was falling all over the camp. The guards yelled at us to run and find cover. Later, we were told that the B-24 crew had bailed out.

From time to time, Sgt. Hasselmann would be accompanied by his Italian girlfriend, Freida Dugar. After the war, she was tried as a collaborator by the Italians. She wrote letters to me, John and Lorin asking for our help. I turned the letter over to the State Department.

A few days later, we were on the road to Verona, Italy. Our destination was a Luftwasser Air Field on the outskirts of the city. It was the first time I saw a 262 German Jet. Sixteen-year-old pilot trainees flew these aircraft. They didn't engage our fighter planes. Fortunately for our Air Force, Germany could not produce too many of these jets. There were two basic ways to down this fighter. One was to get high above it and dive down at full throttle. The other was to catch them when they took off or landed. The flying range of the 262 jet was limited.

As fellow airmen, we were treated with respect by the Luftwasser. Each of us had our own room in a low-level wooden barrack that was at the farthest end of the field. I think we ate the same food as the Germans. I vaguely remember having eggs. After several days, a German corporal led a squad of Wermacht soldiers to our barrack. The men were in their forties and fifties, old enough to be our fathers. They had been fighting on the Russian front and looked tired and defeated. They would escort us to the prisoner of war camps in Germany, called Stalags. We would need protection from irate citizenry as we went through the many towns on our way north to Germany. I had heard about airmen who were shot down being butchered by the townspeople. Daylight bombing had destroyed their towns and killed many, many loved ones.

Each of us was given a suitcase weighing 40 or 50 pounds, filled with grain to carry to Germany. We were separated into several small groups. The officers and Ed Linnane were assigned to one group. The remaining soldiers were split into two other groups. Our destination was Germany via the Brenner Pass and Austria. We had to be on the alert for American fighter planes. The 9th Air Force P-47 Thunderbolts and P-38 Lightnings would escort the bombers to target, then break away and strafe targets of opportunity or "anything that moved." The pilots didn't know if we were American POW's or German troops. I can't remember how many times I dove for the brushes or trees along the sides of the road when we heard the roar of fighter planes.

It didn't take long before blisters formed on my feet from walking in soft felt slippers. After the second day on the road, my feet felt like they were on fire. I started to fall behind the others. The prisoner of war code of conduct was to attempt to escape. I thought about that as I continued to fall farther back. The dirt road was lined with trees and underbrush. I looked to see if the guards were aware that I was lagging behind. I thought I could make a run for the foliage. OK, now, drop the suitcase and sprint into the trees and bushes. I took two steps and grimaced from the pain in my toe and blistered feet. This is not a good idea. One, I never would make it, and two, if I did, what next? Just then, one of the guards shouted at me. He waved his rifle and motioned for me to catch up. I slowly hobbled, moving the heavy suitcase of grain from left arm to right arm, and moved back to the center of the road. Any further thought of escape was over.

On the long journey north toward the Brenner Pass, we mostly walked and sometimes rode on the back of carts, trains, and trucks run by burning wood. One day, while riding in the back of a horse drawn cart, we started to sing Lilly Marlene with the guards. It seemed odd and at the same time "normal" for Americans and Germans, sworn enemies, to sing together. They call this the Stockholm Syndrome: You form an allegiance with the enemy. I had very mixed feelings about this because I was Jewish, though I am not sure if our guards knew that I was Jewish. They did not treat me any different than the rest of the crew. After the war, I received letters from Willi Lehmkuhl and Peter Amrgein, two of our guards. They lived in Nuremburg. Peter wrote that he was captured by the Russians before he was able to reach his home.

Somewhere south of the Brenner Pass, we were put aboard a passenger train. The suitcases were put in a storage area. John and Lorin were seated across from Ed Linnane and me, with their backs facing the front of the train. All the windows were wide open. Suddenly, the train stopped. The engine was stopped in a tunnel with the rest of the rail cars exposed to be "hit by anything that moves." It was a customary practice to put the engine in the tunnel to protect it from strafing. Suddenly, Lorin looked up, His face went white, his jaw dropped. Ed and I took one look and immediately dove out of the window. John and Lorin followed. Two P-47s dipped their wings as they passed over the tunnel. They were so low, for a split second, I could see the pilots' faces. I ran as fast as I could into the tunnel. Fear trumps the severe pain from the burning, blistered feet. I caught my breath. A cold sweat broke out on my forehead. My clothes were soaking wet. I looked at the others. Our eyes spoke of another "pocked marked grey wall." After the attack, we boarded the train again and resumed our trip north toward the Brenner Pass and Austria.

The Brenner Pass was a prime target that had been bombed many times by my 463rd BG. It was a major rail marshalling yard for supplies from Germany, Austria into Italy. After a raid, the Germans would have tracks down and trains running in 20 minutes. The Germans were ingenious. Too bad this ingenuity wasn't used to help mankind instead of destroying it. After we disembarked, the guards escorted us through the Pass. I saw bombed out buildings, rubble in the streets, and many bomb craters. Most of the people in the area were military. The anti-aircraft batteries were manned by young Nazis who made it clear that they were winning the war.

As we marched, it was difficult to walk in a straight line because of the destruction the bombings had inflicted on the Pass. Recessed between the bombed buildings was a low concrete shelter with a large Red Cross sign. Our guards motioned for us to enter. Two German SS soldiers blocked the door. A heated argument ensued which was won by the SS. Our guards motioned for us to continue on to the nearby train station. We joined other Germans and boarded a steam engine train to Munich. We entered a first class compartment that had two long benches covered with a deep red velvet material. The benches faced each other and accommodated eight people. The seven of us, four American prisoners and three German guards, joined a German Major already seated at the window.

The German Major looked to be in his mid-forties. His tailored uniform fit snugly on his solid frame. He had a monocle in his right eye and a scar across his right cheek. He was a poster boy for what a Heidelberg Officer should look like. In broken English, with tears in his eyes, he pleaded with us to tell the American Army to join forces with the Germans and fight the Russians. The Germans were deathly afraid of the Russians. They had brutalized them earlier in the war. They knew the Russians would retaliate in kind. We looked at our guards who gave us an eye sign to ignore the remarks.

The Austrian countryside was beautiful. There were few signs of the war. We passed through undulating green hills and manicured farms. The barn designs were in Germanic style, a sharp contrast to the Italian farms and landscape. We arrived in Munich about 4:00 p.m. We waited for the train to empty and then followed the guards to the far end of the platform.

Again, as at the Brenner Pass, we walked through the war torn streets of Munich. The city was almost completely destroyed by the constant bombings, the Americans by day and the British by night. We arrived at a large hotel that seemed to have little damage. The lobby was crowded with mostly military people. We entered through a side door to prevent another incident like the one at the Brenner Pass. The guards took us to a large room where we would spend the night. As we entered the room, the air raid sirens went off. We were led down a stairwell to a sub cellar. It was very crowded with other hotel residents.

I could hear the bombs explode and felt the ground shake. I remember lying on the cold marble floor. I actually bounced from the concussions. I looked up, and standing over me was a very, very tall man in Arabic garb with a tunic headdress. He had the blackest eyes I have ever seen or will ever see. They were like lasers. He looked down at me with utter contempt. I am not sure if he stared at me because I was an American flyer or because I was a Jewish American flyer. After 30 minutes, the sirens sounded the all clear.

The next day, we were split up. The officers were sent to Stalag 13D in Nuremberg. The enlisted men were sent to Stalag 7A in Moosberg. Our guards told us that they are being replaced. They were relieved to be able to go home to find their families.

Another day, another walk. For me, it was another day of hobbling. The pain from my blistered feet was agonizing. More dirt roads, more scanning the skies for American fighter planes out to hit "anything that moves." We arrived at Nuremberg, and like Munich, it was almost totally destroyed by the bombings. When it rained, there were very few houses that didn't leak. We left the city center and finally arrived at the high barbed wire fence of Stalag 13D. This would be "home" until April 25, 1945.

CHAPTER SEVEN

Stalag13D was originally a prisoner of war camp for the Italians. I was told that living conditions then were subhuman. At times, the compound had as many as 10,000 inmates. By April 1945, the number was down to a just a few thousand. Most of the Americans were transferred to Stalag 7A in Moosberg. 13D was surrounded by a double row of barbed wire fences. Towers were manned by Germans with 50-caliber machine guns spaced strategically around the compound. The wooden barracks had stoves but varied in the numbers of bays and beds. Latrines were in a separate building with open trenches. The smell was overpowering. I lost track of time.

After I was deloused, I joined the other POWs. Most were Americans, some were British, and a few were French and Serbians. The food was limited to hot cabbage or potato soup with black bread and ersatz coffee. We were given Red Cross packages that had powdered milk, chocolate, nuts, raisins, tins of spam and beans and a can opener. I still have the can opener attached to my dog tags. Trading for food was very common. Cigarettes commanded the highest price. I learned how to make an "energy bar" from powdered milk, chocolate, and anything else that was available. It tasted great and had the effect of a "power bar."

I found a Serbian "doctor" who cut open my silver dollar blisters. I sat outdoors on a wooden table with my feet extended, gripping the edge of the table in sheer agony. I had to keep off my feet for several days and let the air and sun heal the soles. Fortunately, the soles did not become infected. Somewhere, somehow, someone located a pair of GI boots. I couldn't put them on until my feet healed. I know it saved my feet.

Excitement ran high when we heard through the grapevine that Patton's 3rd Army was approaching. On or about April 25, the siege of Nuremberg began. In the early afternoon of April 25th, German guards ordered John, Lorin and me to follow them to one of the exit gates. We were joined by 15 other Americans and one Frenchman. A German colonel came out followed by a captain and 23 guards. We were told to form two lines. The gate opened and we started walking. My feet ached, as they were not completely healed. I was very apprehensive. Where were we going? Why me? Why us?

We started walking on the road south. It was the only direction left open. Halftracks, tanks and artillery started to shell the city. The din was deafening. The ground shook from the shelling. Night had fallen. We could hear the American fighter planes engaging the German

109 Messerchmitts above us. I could actually hear the different sounds of the fighter planes. Tracer bullets lit up the sky. The smell of the cordite clogged my nose and throat.

No one was sure when the Colonel and the Captain left the detail. It would later turn out to be a blessing. We passed Tiger tanks with the dreaded 88mm guns protruding from the turrets. They were huge, noisy, cumbersome machines. Their tracks cut into the dirt road leaving deep ridges. Although less maneuverable, there armament and firepower were far superior to the Sherman Tank. The most effective way to destroy them was by tracer fire from a P-47 hitting the rear engine.

After two hours on the road, I collapsed from the pain in my raw feet. The guards prodded me with their bayonets. "Arouse! Schnell!" they yelled, sticking the point of the bayonet in my thigh. The French airman told the sergeant in German, "You can shoot him or leave him, but he cannot go on!" I could understand what they were saying. Frankly, the pain was so great I didn't give a damn. Someone in the group started to talk to the Sergeant that the war was lost. He should give up. We would tell the Americans that they were only following orders. They would be fed and well taken care of. After a short pause, he agreed. We could see a farmhouse off to the right of the road. Quickly, we left the road. Somehow, I was able to limp along to reach the farmhouse. There was only the German farmer and his wife. He offered us his house and food.

I could hear heavy artillery and tank gunfire. From the upstairs window, I could see the German Army retreating. If the Germans found us, they would kill us all, Americans and Germans alike. We made a mad dash to the barn. I tunneled under the hay to wait out the retreating Germans. I could hear them in the farmyard. Several came into the barn and poked around with their bayonets. Luckily, no one was hurt. I waited until I heard only the creaking of the wooden barn siding. Slowly, I shed the hay and poked my head out of the barn door. It was clear and quiet. I decided to return to the house. John and Lorin along with some of the others decided to remain in the barn.

The shelling increased in intensity. The 86th Blackhawk Division of the Third Army zeroed in the crossroads in the town just south of the farmhouse. The pounding was so severe I thought the ceiling would collapse. I went down into the wine cellar with some of the guards. The cellar was only six feet high. I instinctively held my hands over my head to support floor beams. I foolishly thought I could stop those beams from collapsing. Some of the guards did the same. The bombardment went on all night. No one slept. I am not sure how I was able to stand in this position for so many hours.

At about 5 o'clock in the morning, the shelling stopped. I came upstairs and peeked out of the windows. I could hear the rumble of the halftracks. I could see movement and dust swirls coming from the north. A halftrack appeared over the crest of the road. We all came out into the farmyard. Some POWs grabbed the Germans' rifles. Someone else grabbed a pitchfork and put a white cloth on it. He started to wave the flag. We shouted, "We are Americans! We are Americans!"

What a sight. Everywhere the eye could see were American halftracks, Jeeps, and GIs. A squad of GIs came into the farmyard. We turned the Germans over to them. We told them that we had promised them they would be fed and treated fairly. We became POWs again. But this was by the USA 3rd Army, 86th Blackhawk Division. We were then transported to the 86th Blackhawk Division Headquarters in an old castle south of Nuremburg.

It was April 26, 1945. I had been a prisoner of war held by the enemy for 36 days.

CHAPTER EIGHT

Repatriated Americans were held as prisoners until verification of name, rank and serial number. This was necessary because many Germans soldiers would masquerade as American GIs to avoid capture. The men of the 86th Blackhawk Division were a mixture of veterans that had landed in Normandy and new recruits. Some platoons, like E Platoon had a one hundred and fifty percent turnover. They were tough, hardened combat soldiers that would kill Germans without batting an eye and come to tears when they saw children starving.

We were the best-treated prisoners of war ever while we stayed in the old castle manned by the 86th. The upper two floors of the castle stored contraband the Germans had "captured": sterling silverware, oil paintings, furniture, satin and silk sheets and other items too numerous to name. It was Bergdorf Goodman without departments. I took several pairs of silk stockings. I thought they would come in handy or I'd give them to my mother. I found an old German typewriter and wrote a letter to my family. The letter was dated April 26, 1945. I told them that all our crew was OK. We took twenty-three Germans as prisoners. All nineteen POWs were safe.

It took several days later for Army Intelligence (G2) to clear and debrief us. We told them about the Tiger Tanks and the location of the 88mm anti-aircraft gun on the road from Nuremberg.

John, Lorin and I were issued open travel orders. We could go anywhere we wanted. I could have seen all of Europe, but my mind was on getting home as fast as I could. I am not sure of the sequence that got me to Paris. It was on to Weisbaden, then Frankfurt, where I boarded a C-47 flight to Paris. We flew at about 500 feet in one of the worst storms I can remember. The C-47 was buffeted by gale like winds. Rain pounded the windows and fuselage. Both pilots had to hold the yoke with both hands to keep the plane level. Visibility was at a minimum. The plane bounced as if we were on a trampoline. I held onto the overhead spar as the plane yawed, dipped and fishtailed. The engines strained to keep full power. I wondered how in the world the pilot would be able to land at Orly Field. I thought of asking John and Lorin to take over. The landing was relatively smooth given the weather conditions. These pilots were good.

I spent a couple of days in Paris. Yes, the silk stockings were very useful in Paris. Then I moved on to Dieppe, where a steamer would take me to Dover. The North Sea was very choppy with ten-foot waves. I remained in my bunk and was serenaded by the ships engines. The drone seemed to have a singsong melody. Every time the ship went up the tone went lower. This pattern reversed as the bow would plunge into the waves. I went topside in the late afternoon. In the distance, I could see the white cliffs of Dover. From Dover, we were trucked to a hotel in downtown London.

London was still under attack from V-2 rockets. The number of rockets per day had dropped considerably but still the sirens went off several times each day. It was amazing to see buildings standing intact next to partially or completely destroyed buildings. Rubble was swept to the side of the streets for removal by a special home security corps. When the sirens went off, I left my fourth floor hotel room and, along with other Americans, followed the Brits down the stairwell. The hotel was a short distance from the Underground. We jogged across the avenue. There was no stampede or panic. It was just like a double time drill in boot camp

One by one, quickly, but under control, I went down the stone stairs that wound down to the fourth level. This was old hat to the Brits. For me, I was again as scared as I was in the sub-basement of the Munich hotel when American B-17's and B-24's dropped their bombs on the city. The Brits took out their daily papers, some played cards, and some just dozed off. This was what life had become in London since 1939. They were no different than my fellow POWs who had been imprisoned in POW camps. Human beings do adapt to their surroundings. It's a no brainer: Adapt or die.

On May 8, 1945, after six years of war, the British people released all of their pent up emotions that were held in check for so many years. The Londoners cried, laughed, danced, sang. Some expressed all of these emotions all at the same time. Hugs and kisses were the order of the day. Trafalgar Square was jam packed, like the throngs in Times Square watching the ball drop to welcome the New Year. There were no "enemies." The terrible, costly ordeal was over. No more German bombs or V rockets, fires, rationing, dark curtains, hiding in the lowest depth of the underground. Now the "boys" would be coming home. There will be a new beginning.

The next day a victory parade was held. All the pomp and circumstances was called out. The King and Queen in that special carriage, Winston Churchill, and every lord and Member of

Parliament. The streets were jam-packed. I was standing next to Londoners who were whooping and waving: "No greater love have they," or words like that. I asked them why they loved their Royalty. In their mind, they identified with them. It didn't matter whether they were firemen, cooks, bottle washers. Seeing Royalty gave them a small piece of being Royalty.

Two days later, I was transported to Southampton to board the Swedish Steamship Stockholm, sister ship of the Gripsholm, to join the last official convoy to leave England. Now she would become another transport in the last official convoy to sail to New York Harbor. She would carry over 1,000 American servicemen and servicewomen that had survived the war, a mixture of POWs, amputees, injured and hospitalized GIs.

The first day out, the Stockholm hit a severe storm. Twenty-foot waves tossed the ship like a toy in a child's tub. It reminded me of the Cyclone, a roller coaster ride in Coney Island, New York. The bow would drop down leaving an empty pit in my stomach and then rise up so that the rudder would hover in the air. I think this was where Rock and Roll was invented. The only way to stave off seasickness was to go topside and weather the wind, rain and spray. I faced away from the wind to ease my breathing. As I held on to the starboard railing, my mind wandered back to my first meeting with John Lincoln and Crew 11-30.

CHAPTER NINE

The next morning the stormy seas quieted down. The clouds drifted eastward. The sun rose slowly over the horizon with the bow of the Stockholm pointed directly into its center. It reminded me of a giant orange lollipop with the ship, the stick.

The days passed slowly. I can't recall the food, roll calls, accommodations, card games, or guys sunning on the deck. I wrote letters to be mailed when we landed. Day passed into night and then to day again. The continued use of blackout curtains was a constant reminder that the war was not over. There was concern that a German submarine may not have received the notice of Germany's surrender.

On the third night out the Stockholm slowed down. The crew passed the word that we were off Sandy Hook. We anchored the ship so we could sail up the Hudson Bay into the New York harbor the next morning. The blackout curtains were stored and all the ship lights came on. The war was truly over in Europe. After breakfast, we steamed into the lower Hudson Bay. The cheering turned into a roar. Then, as if on cue, the roaring stopped as we approached the Statue of Liberty. Everyone who could went to the port side of the ship. Others who could not were carried to the railing. Only, the bedridden stayed below. The only audible sound was the steady hum of the diesel engines, the swish of the water as the bow cut through the green murky water, and my heartbeat. Tugboats came up on either side of the ship. The cheering and whooping began again. Slowly, the tugs guided the ship into a berth in the forties and Twelfth Avenue. Shouts were exchanged with the sailors and longshoremen: names, where are you from, etc. We gave the crew letters for mailing and phone numbers to call. I made it home, a bit bruised with emotional baggage that would take me 50 years to recognize, but in one piece.

I was bussed down to Atlantic City, New Jersey, about three hours south of New York City. It was the same city where I took basic training so long ago. I was not the same person that walked the boardwalk to Glenn Miller's music. This time I walked leisurely over to the Traymore Hotel to see the room I had shared with other Army Air Corps cadets. Now, it was a hospital for amputees. The Air Corps had taken over many hotels and converted them into hospitals. As I entered the lobby with the Art Deco walls, all I could see were amputees. I momentarily stared at these soldiers. Any thought of going up the elevator to my old room disappeared.

I spent the next few days doing paperwork and undergoing physical exams. None of us would admit that we had physical or emotional problems. I was told that I would be getting a 60-day leave and that upon my return I would be sent to the 20th Air Force in the Pacific. I am not sure how I got back to Brooklyn. I remember walking from the subway station at New Utrecht and 45th Street along 41st Street. There was a snafu with communications. My family did not know that I was coming home this day. The celebration began for several days. My over eighty year old grandmother told me she ran the eight blocks in pouring rain to my aunt's house, clutching the telegram from the War Department in her hand, saying I was safe.

While I was on leave, I received the letter I had written on April 26 to my family from the 86th Blackhawk Headquarters. I actually beat the mail home. I was still on leave on August 6, 1945, when the first atomic bomb was dropped on Hiroshima. Three days later, on August 9, 1945, the second atomic bomb was dropped on Nagasaki. President Truman gave the order. It was a very difficult and agonizing decision, but I believe it was the right decision. It ended the war and saved millions of American and Japanese lives. There is no question that the Japanese people, led by their fanatical War Lords, would have fought to their death to protect their homeland. This was clearly demonstrated by the Japanese troops that would not surrender on Iwo Jima.

I returned from leave to Fort Dix, New Jersey. A discharge point system had been posted. POWs were given an additional five points. This made me eligible for discharge. On August 11, 1945, I became a civilian. I could have stayed in the Army Air Corps and would have been promoted, but I didn't think I could survive two wars. I ran to enlist, and now I ran to be discharged. First Lt. Moe Wolf, my new brother-in-law (who flew 50 missions as a B-24 bombardier in 1942 when his 376 Bomber Group was based in Bengharzy, Libya), drove my folks and sister to Fort Dix to pick me up. When he needed directions to leave the base, I told him to turn right and pointed left. So much for my navigation skills.

CHAPTER TEN

The greatest legislation ever passed was the G.I. Bill of Rights. President Roosevelt created this program midway through the war. He would not make the mistakes and false promises of World War I. Those returning servicemen were not given bonuses or given medical treatment, which in turn triggered the great march on the Capitol that resulted in deaths and jail sentences for the participants. The GI Bill opened the college doors to all veterans. Hundreds of thousands of young men took this opportunity to get college degrees. This resulted in creating the greatest wealth this country had ever achieved. Yes, we became the "Greatest Generation."

I had problems adjusting to civilian life and, in particular, college. I didn't realize that the stress of being a prisoner of war had affected my behavior. The Veterans Administration did not recognize Post Traumatic Stress Syndrome (PTSD) as an illness at that time. Thanks to another Harvey, Harvey Brock, a cousin by marriage, I was able to matriculate and graduate with a degree in Industrial Engineering from New York University. After a failed marriage, I spent the next 20 years playing "catch-up." I got lucky in 1966 when I met Minerva. In early 1967, we married. After 42 years, the honeymoon goes on. I spent 35 years in the plastic/textile business. I was able to marry my metal working background with plastics and textiles to develop many synthetic products. I retired in 1988 as Vice President of Troy Products, a subsidiary of Troy Mills, Troy, New Hampshire. My life has had many ups and downs. The ups were a great family life while growing up, the Army Air Corps experience, a successful career in plastic/textiles, and a great marriage to Minerva, her son Jamie and my three grandchildren: Jason, Jennifer and Christopher. The downs were being a prisoner of war, one failed marriage, and the death of my son at an early age. On balance, it could have been worse.

Crew 11-30

Back, from left to right: Herbert Wagner, Oren Herick, Lewis Brown, Ed Linnane, Michael Brown.

Front, from left to right: John Lincoln, Harvey Horn, George Kall, Lorin Millard.

Leroy Swindlehurst (left) and Dan Balik (right)

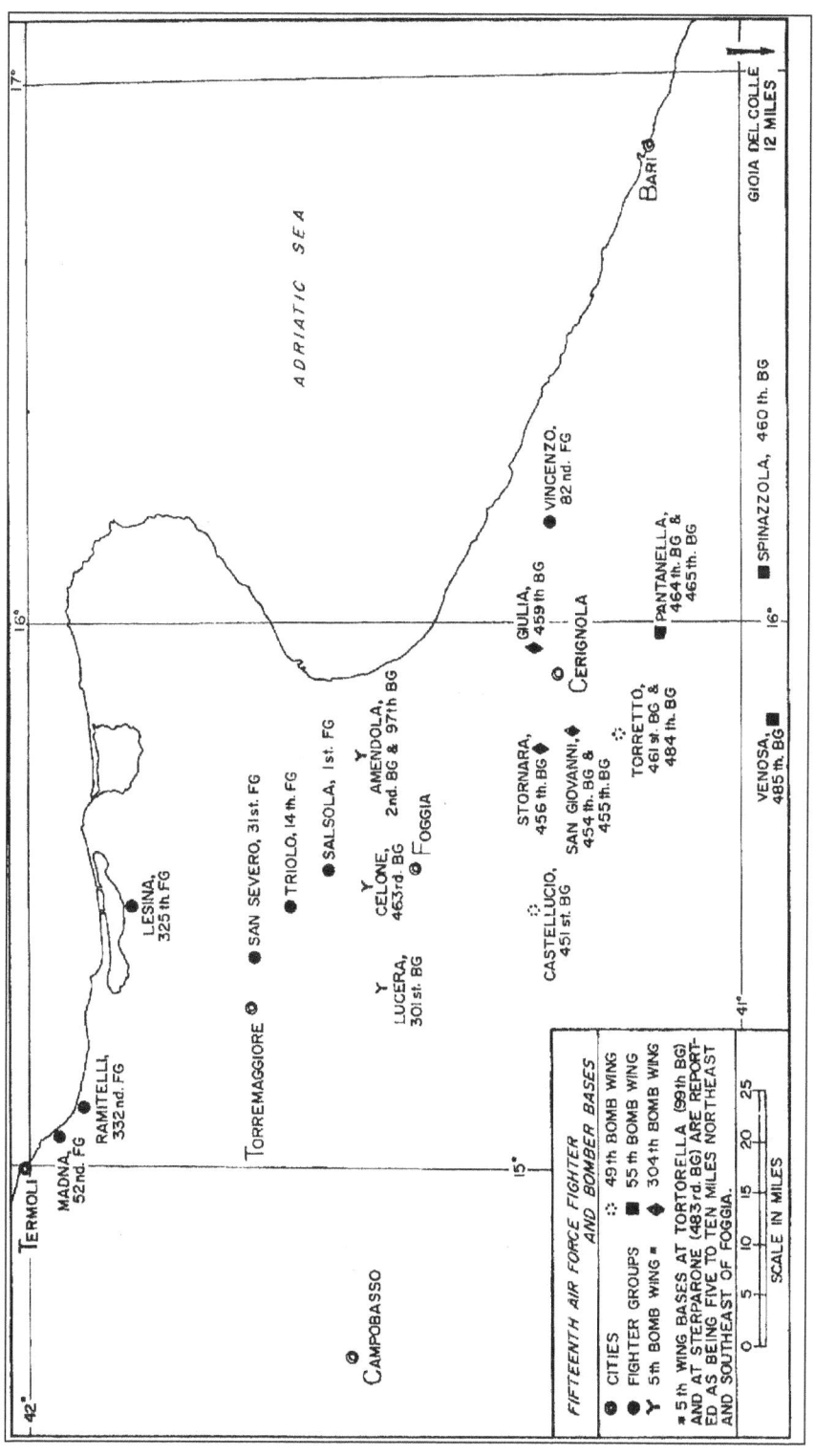

463rd Bomb Group Missions

AC/Lost

0 3/18/44 U/1 Villa Orba, Italy, with 2nd BG
00 3/19/44 U/2 Klagenfurt, Germ., with 97th BG
1 3/30/44 39/0 A/D Imotsky, Yugo.
2 4/2/44 34/0 M/Y Brod, Yugo.
3 4/3/44 38/0 M/Y Brod, Yugo.
4 4/5/44 38/0 M/Y Nis, Yugo.
5 4/6/44 38/2 A/D Zagreb, Yugo.
6 4/7/44 35/1 M/Y Treviso, Italy
7 4/12/44 37/0 AC/F Fishamend-Markt, Aust.
8 4/13/44 32/0 AC/F Gyor, Hung.
9 4/15/44 36/0 M/Y Ploesti, Rum. Bombs not dropped.
10 4/16/44 35/0 A/D F or M/Y Belgrade, Yugo.
11 4/17/44 35/0 M/Y Belgrade, Yugo.
12 4/20/44 34/0 M/Y Vicenza, Italy. Bombs not dropped.
13 4/23/44 35/0 AC/F Wiener Neustadt, Aust.
14 4/24/44 36/1 M/Y Ploesti, Rum.
15 4/28/44 37/0 Docks Piombino, Italy
16 4/29/44 27/1 Sub Pens Toulon, France
17 4/30/44 34/1 AC/F Varese, Italy
18 5/5/44 35/4 O/R Ploesti, Rum.
19 5/6/44 35/0 O/R Brasov, Rum.
20 5/7/44 45/0 M/Y Bucharest, Rum.
21 5/10/44 34/7 Wiener Neustadt (1 listd Vienna)
22 5/12/44 35/0 Elba Isle Docks Portoferraio, Italy
23 5/13/44 36/0 M/Y Trento, Italy
24 5/14/44 33/0 A/D Piacenza, Italy
25 5/18/44 35/6 Rum. Romano-Amer. O/R Ploesti, Rum.
26 5/19/44 26/0 O/S Portomaggiore, Italy
27 5/22/44 26/0 M/Y Avezzano, Italy
28 5/24/44 31/0 Azgersdorf A/CF Vienna, Aust.
29 5/26/44 29/0 M/Y Saint-Etienne, Fr.
30 5/27/44 31/0 M/Y Avignon, Fr.
31 5/29/44 28/0 Wallersdorf A/D Wiener Neustadt, Aust.
32 5/30/44 28/0 M/Y Zagreb, Yugo.
33 5/31/44 27/0 O/R Ploiste, Rum.
34 6/2/44 27/1 M/Y Oradea, Rum.
35 6/4/44 27/0 Var River Bridge, Nice, Fr.
36 6/5/44 27/1 Reno River RR Bridge Pioppi Viaduct, Italy
37 6/6/44 28/1 M/Y Belgrade, Yugo
38 6/8/44 27/0 Sub/B Pola, Italy
39 6/9/44 28/0 A/D Oberpaffenhoffen, Germ.
40 6/10/44 27/1 Porto Marghera M/Y Mestre, Italy
41 6/11/44 27/0 M/Y Smederevo, Yugo.
42 6/13/44 25/1 A/D Oberpaffenhoffen
43 6/14/44 27/3 O/R Budapest, Hung.
44 6/16/44 23/1 Kagran-Vacuum O/R Vienna, Aust.
45 6/22/44 26/0 M/Y Modena, Italy
46 6/23/44 27/0 O/R Ploesti, Rum.
47 6/25/44 27/1 M/Y Sete, Fr.
48 6/26/44 26/0 O/R Vienna, Aust.
49 6/27/44 25/1 M/Y Budapest, Hung.
50 6/30/44 25/0 A/D Banja Luka, Yugo.
51 7/2/44 24/0 Almes Fuzito O/R Dunaalbas, Aust. *
52 7/4/44 24/0 Photogen O/R Brasov, Rum.
53 7/5/44 27/0 M/Y Montelier, Fr.
54 7/6/44 26/0 Steel/F Bergamo, Italy
55 7/7/44 26/4 O/S Blechhammer, Germ.
56 7/8/44 24/3 Zwolfaxen A/D Vienna, Aust.
57 7/9/44 21/0 O/R Ploesti, Rum.
58 7/13/44 24/0 M/Y Verona, Italy

* 463rd History shows target at Budapest, Hung.

59 7/14/44 25/1 M/Y Budapest, Hung.
60 7/15/44 25/0 O/R Ploesti, Rum.
61 7/16/44 27/0 Winterhoffen O/D Vienna, Aust.
62 7/18/44 25/0 A/D Memmingen, Germ.
53 7/19/44 25/1 Milbershofen O/R Munich, Germ.
64 7/20/44 27/0 A/D Memmingen, Germ.
65 7/21/44 26/0 S/O Brux, Czech.
66 7/22/44 24/0 O/R Ploesti, Rum.
67 7/24/44 25/0 Tank Repair Works Turin, Italy
68 7/25/44 27/2 Herman Goring-Tank Works, Linz, Aust.
69 7/26/44 21/0 A/C Fact. Wiener-Neudorf, Aust.
70 7/28/44 23/1 O/R Ploesti, Rum.
71 7/30/44 26/0 M/Y Brod, Yugo.
72 7/31/44 25/1 Xenia O/R Ploesti, Rum.
73 8/3/44 21/0 Oberraderach Hydrogen/F Friedrichshafen, Ger.
74 8/6/44 27/0 Bridge Le Pouzin, France
75 8/7/44 26/0 South S/O Blechhammer, Germ.
76 8/9/44 28/0 A/C Component Fact. Gyor, Hung.
77 8/10/44 27/0 O/R Ploesti, Rum.
78 8/12/44 20/0 Shore Guns Savona, Italy
79 8/13/44 24/0 Shore Guns Savona, Italy
80 8/14/44 27/0 Shore Guns St. Raphael, France
81 8/15/44 28/4 Bridge Valence, France
82 8/17/44 23/1 A/D Nis, Yugo
83 8/18/44 27/0 Romano-Americano O/R Ploesti, Rum.
84 8/19/44 24/1 Xenia O/R Ploesti, Rum.
85 8/22/44 26/2 O/R Blechhammer, Germ. (Secondary target)
86 8/23/44 24/6 A/C Fact. Wiener-Neustadt, Aust.
87 8/24/44 28/0 A/D Pardurice, Czech.
88 8/25/44 27/0 A/D Brno, Czech.
89 8/26/44 28/0 RR Bridge Aviso, Italy
90 8/27/44 28/0 North O/R Blechhammer, Germ.
91 8/28/44 28/0 Moosbierbaum, Aust.
92 8/29/44 28/0 O/R Bohumin, Czech.
93 8/30/44 28/1 M/Y Novi Sad, Yugo.
94 9/1/44 28/0 RR Bridge Tesica Morava, Yugo.
95 9/3/44 27/0 Sava River RR Bridge Belgrade, Yugo.
96 9/4/44 28/0 Sub Pens Genoa, Italy
97 9/5/44 28/0 RR Bridge Budapest, Hung.
98 9/6/44 28/0 RR Bridge Oradea, Rum.
99 9/8/44 28/0 RR Bridge Brod, Yugo & M/Y Sarajevo, Yugo.
100 9/10/44 28/0 Schwecat O/R Vienna, Aust.
101 9/12/44 28/1 Lechfeld A/D Munich, Germ.
102 9/13/44 28/2 O/R Blechhammer, Germ.
103 9/15/44 27/0 Kalamaki A/D Athens, Greece
104 9/17/44 26/0 M/Y Budapest, Hung.
105 9/18/44 28/0 RR Bridge Novi Sad, Yugo.
106 9/20/44 28/0 RR Brdg. Szob, Hung. (Some lists show Budapest)
107 9/21/44 28/0 M/Y Bekescaba, Hung.
108 9/22/44 27/0 Allach BMW Motor Works Munich, Germ.
109 9/23/44 27/1 S/O Brux, Czech.
110 10/4/44 12/0 RR Bridge Pordenone, Italy
111 10/4/44 23/0 M/Y Munich, Germ.
112 10/7/44 24/0 Lobau O/R Vienna, Aust.
113 10/7/44 13/0 M/Y Nove Zamky, Hung.
114 10/10/44 28/0 M/Y Porto Marghera/Mestre, Italy
115 10/11/44 18/0 Motor Works Graz, Aust.
116 10/12/44 36/1 Bivouac Area Bologna, Italy
117 10/13/44 22/0 South O/R Blechhammer, Germ.
118 10/13/44 18/2 Florisdorf O/R Vienna, Aust.
119 10/14/44 33/0 M/Y Nove Zamky, Hung.

#	Date	Mission	Target
120	10/16/44	36/0	Area Bombing Linz, Aust.
121	10/17/44	28/1	South O/R Blechhammer, Germ.
122	10/20/44	35/0	O/S Regensburg, Germ.
123	10/23/44	34/0	Target Unlisted Plaven, Germ.
124	10/25/44	1/0	A/C Factory Klagenfurt, Germ.
125	10/26/44	2/0	M/Y Innsbruck, Aust.
126	10/28/44	2/0	West M/Y Munich, Germ. (1 lists Klagenfurt)
127	11/2/44	3/0	O/R Moosbierbaum, Aust.
128	11/3/44	1/0	South Ord. Depot Vienna, Aust.
129	11/4/44	36/0	Winterhofen O/S Regensburg, Germ.
130	11/5/44	27/0	Florisdorf O/R Vienna, Aust.
131	11/6/44	36/0	Strashoff M/Y Deutsch Wagram, Aust.
132	11/7/44	26/0	M/Y Maribor, Yugo.
133	11/7/44	3/0	Florisdorf O/R Vienna, Aust.
134	11/11/44	31/0	M/Y Salzburg, Aust.
135	11/12/44	2/0	South O/R Blechhammer, Germ.
136	11/15/44	3/0	Benzol O/R Linz, Aust.
137	11/16/44	35/1	M/Y Innsbruck, Aust.
138	11/17/44	32/0	M/Y Salzburg, Aust.
139	11/18/44	35/0	O/R Vienna, Aust.
140	11/18/44	8/0	No target listed Visegrad, Yugo.
141	11/19/44	27/0	Winterhofen O/S Vienna, Aust.
142	11/20/44	35/0	M/Y Brno, Czech.
143	11/22/44	36/0	West M/Y Munich, Germ.
144	11/24/44	6/0	Benzol Ref. Lenz, Aust.
145	11/30/44	2/0	Benzol Ref. Lenz, Aust.
146	12/7/44	1/0	No target listed Spittel, Aust.
147	12/8/44	3/0	O/R Moosbierbaum, Aust.
148	12/9/44	36/2	M/Y Regensburg, Germ.
149	12/12/44	6/1	South O/R Blechhammer, Germ.
150	12/18/44	34/0	O/R Odertal, Germ.
151	12/19/44	37/0	Sopom M/Y Vienna, Aust.
152	12/20/44	35/1	O/S Regensburg, Germ.
153	12/25/44	27/1	South O/R Brux, Czech.
154	12/26/44	27/0	O/R Odertal, Germ.
155	12/27/44	33/1	M/Y Linz, Aust.
156	12/28/44	16/0	O/S Regensburg, Germ.
157	12/29/44	29/0	M/Y Innsbruk, Aust./Udine, Italy
158	1/15/45	26/1	S.E. M/Y Vienna, Aust.
159	1/20/45	28/0	O/R Regensburg Germ. & M/Y Salsburg, Germ.
160	1/21/45	21/0	Lobau O/R Vienna, Aust.
161	1/31/45	28/0	O/R Moosbierbaum, Aust.
162	2/1/45	34/0	M/Y Graz, Aust.
163	2/5/45	36/0	O/S Regensburg, Germ.
164	2/7/45	33/1	Schwecat O/R Vienna, Aust.
165	2/8/45	25/0	Ord. Works Vienna, Aust.
166	2/9/45	3/0	O/R Moosbierbaum, Aust.
167	2/13/45	38/1	Supply Depot Vienna, Aust.
168	2/14/45	40/0	Labau O/R Vienna, Aust.
169	2/15/45	41/1	S.E. Goods Depot Vienna, Aust.
170	2/16/45	40/2	M/Y Bolzano, Italy
171	2/17/45	28/0	Main M/Y Linz, Aust.
172	2/18/45	26/0	M/Y Linz, Aust.
173	2/19/45	26/0	M/Y Klagenfurt, Germ.
174	2/20/45	26/0	Schwecat O/R Vienna, Aust.
175	2/21/45	26/1	M/Y & Shops Vienna, Aust.
176	2/22/45	25/0	Com. Immernstadt & Weiheim, Germ. *
177	2/23/45	28/0	M/Y Bruck, Aust.
178	2/24/45	20/0	M/Y Klagenfurt, Aust.
179	2/25/45	26/2	M/Y Linz, Aust.
180	2/27/45	27/1	M/Y Augsburg, Germ.
181	2/28/45	40/0	Perona RR Bridge Verona, Italy
182	3/1/45	41/1	O/R Moosbierbaum, Aust.
183	3/2/45	27/0	M/Y Linz, Aust.
184	3/4/45	39/0	M/Y Zagreb, Yugo. & Knittelfield, Aust.
185	3/8/45	40/0	M/Y Hegeysholom, Hung.
186	3/9/45	45/1	M/Y Graz, Aust.
187	3/10/45	21/0	Perona RR Bridge Verona, Italy
188	3/12/45	42/0	Florisdorf O/R Vienna, Aust.
189	3/13/45	24/0	M/Y Regensburg, Germ.
190	3/14/45	39/0	O/R Szony, Hung.
191	3/15/45	39/1	O/R Ruhland & Schwartzheide, Germ.
192	3/16/45	33/0	Schweicat O/R Vienna, Aust.
193	3/19/45	42/0	M/Y Landshut, Germ.
194	3/20/45	38/2	Kagran O/R Vienna, Aust. & M/Y Amstettin
195	3/21/45	37/0	Vosendorf O/R Vienna, Aust.
196	3/22/45	27/0	O/R Ruhland & Lauta Alum. Works, Germ.
197	3/23/45	28/1	O/R Ruhland, Germ.
198	3/24/45	20/7	Daimler-Benz Tank Works Berlin, Germ.
199	3/25/45	27/0	Kbely A/D Prague, Czech.
200	3/26/45	28/0	M/Y Wiener Neustadt, Aust.
201	3/30/45	4/0	North Goods Depot Vienna, Aust.
202	3/31/45	25/0	M/Y Linz, Aust.
203	4/1/45	28/0	RR Bridge Maribor, Yugo.
204	4/2/45	28/0	M/Y Graz, Aust.
205	4/5/45	28/1	A/D Udine, Italy
206	4/6/45	28/0	Perona Bridge Verona, Italy
207	4/7/45	28/0	Perona Bridge Verona, Italy
208	4/8/45	28/0	RR Bridge Campodazzo, Italy
209	4/9/45	42/0	Apricot Operations Buckland, Italy
210	4/10/45	42/1	Charlie operations Buckland, Italy
211	4/11/45	28/0	Vipiteno RR Bridge Bolzano, Italy
212	4/12/45	27/0	RR Bridge Padua, Italy
213	4/15/45	39/0	Tactical Target Bologna, Italy
213	4/15/45	20/0	RR Bridge Nervesa, Italy
214	4/17/45	42/0	Ma23 Tactical target Bologna, Italy
215	4/18/45	42/0	Ma23 tactical Target Bolonga, Italy
216	4/19/45	42/0	RR Bridge Inn-Rattenburg, Aust.
217	4/20/45	42/2	M/Y Fortezzo/Brennero, Italy & Innsbruck Aust.
218	4/21/45	28/0	M/Y Rosenheim, Aust.
219	4/23/45	42/0	Hwy. Bridge Bonavigo, Italy
220	4/24/45	41/0	RR Bridges Carsarsa & Malborghetto, Italy
221	4/25/45	27/1	main M/Y Linz, Aust.
222	4/26/45		Ammo. Depot Bronzola Laives, Italy

*Also Neustadt & Landshut, Aust.

DIVIDUAL FLIGHT RECORD   Copy

(1) SERIAL NO. T-131 675 (2) NAME HORN HARVEY S. (3) RANK F/O (4) AGE
(5) PERS. CLASS 17 (6) BRANCH AIR CORPS (7) STATION APO 520
(8) ORGANIZATION ASSIGNED: 15TH AIR FORCE — 5TH COMMAND — 463RD GROUP — 772ND SQUADRON
(9) ORGANIZATION ATTACHED —
(10) PRESENT RATING & DATE: NAV. A/O 8-26-44   (11) ORIGINAL RATING & DATE: SAME
(12) TRANSFERRED FROM —   (13) FLIGHT RESTRICTIONS: NONE
(15) TRANSFERRED TO —   (14) TRANSFER DATE —

(17) MONTH: MARCH

DAY	AIRCRAFT TYPE, MODEL & SERIES	NO. LANDINGS	NIGHT N OR NI	NON-PILOT N
5	B-17G	1		2:20
7	"	1		2:40
15	"	1		9:35
16	"	1		2:10
20	"	1		6:00

MISSING IN ACTION 20 MARCH 1945.

CERTIFIED CORRECT:
William Robinson Jr.
WILLIAM ROBINSON JR.
1ST LT., AIRCORPS
OPERATIONS OFFICER

COLUMN TOTALS: 23:45 / NON

(37) THIS MONTH: 23:45
(38) PREVIOUS MONTHS THIS F.Y.: 252:35
(39) THIS FISCAL YEAR: 276:20
(40) PREVIOUS FISCAL YEARS: 58:35 276:20
(41) TO DATE:

46352	*Lil' Liz*	772	MIA Valence 15 Aug 44. Damaged by flak, crashed at Valence. Anthony Cicconi crew, Lawrence, Sontag, Price, Lieberman (KIA), Forster, Orme (KIA), Kane (KIA), Tintera (KIA). (MACR 7459).
46375		774	To Walnut Ridge 9 Jan 46.
46377	*Pretty Baby's Boys*	772	MIA Vienna 20 Mar 45. Mechanical failure, crashed at Koceuje. John Lincoln crew, Horn, Wagoner, Linnane, Stover, Herrick, Brown, Michel, Caldwell. (MACR 13050).
46381	*Queenie*	775	Crashed 4 Apr 45 on a training mission near Lucera. Donald E Johnson crew, Weide, Knee, Ehinger, Schweiger, Sarrat. All KIA.
46391		773	To Walnut Ridge 10 Jan 46.
46394	*Oh, My Aching Back*	774	MIA Udine 5 Apr 45. Damaged by flak, ditched in Adriatic. Wilbur Wetzel crew, Rummel, Begley, Van Kirk, Steffanelli, Moore, Walmer, McPherson, Puckett, Mitchell. (MACR 13640).
46398	*Bucket Bunny*	775	To Walnut Ridge 18 Dec 45.
46401		774	Severe battle damage 19 Aug 44 at Ploesti. Copilot, bombardier KIA. Landed at Foggia Main. Pilot-Grove. To Walnut Ridge 14 Dec 45.
46402		775	Landed at Zara, Yugoslavia after battle damage on 24 Mar 45 mission to Berlin. Two WIA, two KIA. Crew returned to base in C-47. Pilot-Juracich. To Walnut Ridge 5 Jan 46.
46404		775	To Kingman 19 Dec 45.
46406		772	Salvaged overseas 23 Nov 44.
46409			Also at 97th BG. To Walnut Ridge 10 Dec 45.
46410		774	To Walnut Ridge 4 Jan 46.
46417		774	MIA Lechfeld 12 Sep 44. Damaged by flak, crashed near Munich. Graham Milner crew, Thayer, Seruya, Weitz, Kelley, Herman, Siems, Guderley. (MACR 8360).
46418	*Mary Lou II*	775	MIA Fortezza 20 Apr 45. Damaged by flak, crashed near Merano. Warren Turner crew, Teal, Hitnick, Thayne, Campoli, Horner, Prospero, Sanderson, Elston, Huber. Thayne KIA. (MACR 14020).
46419	*Lil' Liz II*	772	MIA Blechhammer 17 Oct 44. Out of fuel, crashed at Ornis. Pilot-Gail McCoy. (MACR 9210).
46421		773	MIA Vienna 20 Mar 45. Damaged by flak, crashed near Vienna. Samuel Ark crew, Stegink, Cavaliere, Fisher, Dvorak, Fassnacht, Babcock, Wallace, Van Wyk, Jackson. Ark, Stegink, Fisher, Jackson KIA, rest POW. (MACR 13052).
46540			To U.S. 1 Jan 46.

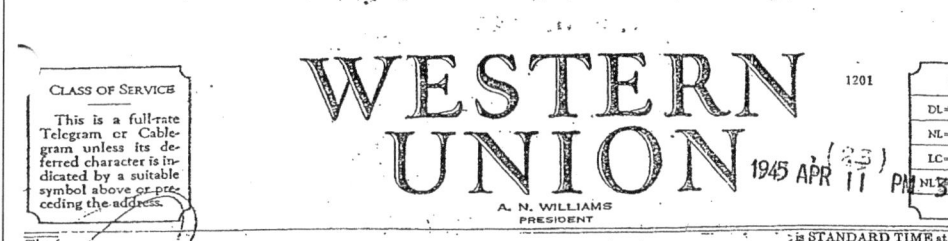

N45 43/42 GOVT=WUX WASHINGTON DC 11 239P

MRS E HORN=
1218 41ST ST=

THE SECRETARY OF WAR DESIRES ME TO EXPRESS HIS DEEP REGRET THAT YOUR SON FLIGHT/OFFICER HORN HARVEY S HAS BEEN MISSING IN ACTION OVER JUGOSLAVIA SINCE 20 MAR 45 IF FURTHER DETAILS OR OTHER INFORMATION ARE RECEIVED YOU WILL BE PROMPTLY NOTIFIED=

ULIO THE ADJUTANT GENERAL.

```
                FIFTEENTH AIR FORCE
              Office of the Commanding General
                     A.P.O. 520
```

3 April 1945

Mrs. Esther Horn
1218 41st Street
Brooklyn, New York

My dear Mrs. Horn:

The news that your son, Flight Officer Harvey S. Horn, T-131675, has been missing in action since March 20, 1945, when the Flying Fortress aboard which he served as the navigator, failed to return from a combat mission to Amstettin, Austria, must have been a great shock to you. Although I can give you no assurance of his safety, I am sure you are interested in the following particulars surrounding his most recent flight.

Information based on the reports of returning airmen reveals that your son's craft became disabled over northern Yugoslavia, and fell out of the formation, losing altitude. When the bomber was last seen it was under good control, leaving the possibility that the crew could have escaped by parachute if that was necessary. Should there be a change in Harvey's status the War Department will notify you without delay.

His personal possessions have been assembled for shipment to the Effects Quartermaster, Army Effects Bureau, Kansas City, Missouri, who will in turn forward them to the designated beneficiary.

Although he was with us but a short time your son has made a vital contribution to the victory toward which we are all striving. You may be very proud of Harvey and the record which he has established.

                              Very sincerely yours,

                              N. F. TWINING
                              Major General, USA
                                 Commanding

WAR DEPARTMENT
THE ADJUTANT GENERAL'S OFFICE
WASHINGTON 25, D. C.

IN REPLY REFER TO:
AG 201 Horn, Harvey S.
PC-N MTO 087

12 April 1945

Mrs. Esther Horn
1218 41st Street
Brooklyn, New York

Dear Mrs. Horn:

    This letter is to confirm my recent telegram in which you were regretfully informed that your son, Flight Officer Harvey S. Horn, T-131675, has been reported missing in action over Jugoslavia since 20 March 1945.

    I realize the distress caused by failure to receive more information or details; therefore, I wish to assure you that in the event additional information is received at any time, it will be transmitted to you without delay. If no information is received in the meantime, I will communicate with you again three months from the date of this letter. It is the policy of the Commanding General of the Army Air Forces, upon receipt of the "Missing Air Crew Report," to convey to you any details that might be contained in that report.

    Inquiries relative to allowances, effects and allotments should be addressed to the agencies indicated in the inclosed Bulletin of Information.

    Permit me to extend to you my heartfelt sympathy during this period of uncertainty.

Sincerely yours,

J. A. ULIO
Major General
The Adjutant General

1 Inclosure
Bulletin of Information

HEADQUARTERS, ARMY AIR FORCES
WASHINGTON

IN REPLY REFER TO: AFPPA-8

AAF 201 (13050) Horn, Harvey S.
T131675

4 May 1945

Mrs. E. Horn
1218 41st Street
Brooklyn, New York

Dear Mrs. Horn:

    I am writing you with reference to your son, Flight Officer Harvey S. Horn, who was reported by The Adjutant General as missing in action over Yugoslavia since 20 March 1945.

    Additional information has been received indicating that Flight Officer Horn was the navigator on a B-17 (Flying Fortress) bomber which departed from Italy on a bombardment mission to Austria on 20 March 1945. The report reveals that during this mission about 2:45 p.m., over Zagreb, Yugoslavia, a radio message was received from your son's bomber stating that it was having difficulty, and that an attempt was being made to reach the coast to make a crash landing. Subsequently his aircraft began to lose altitude, it left the formation, and disappeared from sight. Inasmuch as the crew members of accompanying planes were unable to obtain any other details relative to the loss of Flight Officer Horn's Fortress, the foregoing constitutes all the information presently available.

    Believing you may wish to communicate with the families of the others who were in the plane with your son, I am inclosing a list of these men and the names and addresses of their next of kin.

    Please be assured that a continuing search by land, sea, and air is being made to discover the whereabouts of our missing personnel. As our armies advance over enemy occupied territory, special troops are assigned to this task, and agencies of our government and allies frequently send in details which aid us in bringing additional information to your.

    Very sincerely,

    N. W. Reed

    N. W. REED
    Major, Air Corps
    Assistant Chief, Notification Branch
    Personal Affairs Division
    Assistant Chief of Air Staff, Personnel

1 Incl.

ADDRESS REPLY TO: COMMANDING GENERAL, ARMY AIR FORCES, WASHINGTON 25, D. C.

Pictures and Documents | 56

1. Barracks at Langwasser - Stalag XIII-D
2. Nazis on parade - Nürnberg, 1938
3. You will stand at the Fuehrer's podium
4. The train station at Langwasser
5. Gib (right) at Barracks 23 - Stalag VII-A
6. Nazi Day in Nürnberg, 1934
7. Hitler's Eagle's Nest, above the clouds
8. Museums Bridge - Nürnberg, 1946
9. Tunnel beneath the train station at Langwasser
10. Moosburg a.d. Isar - Stalag VII-A

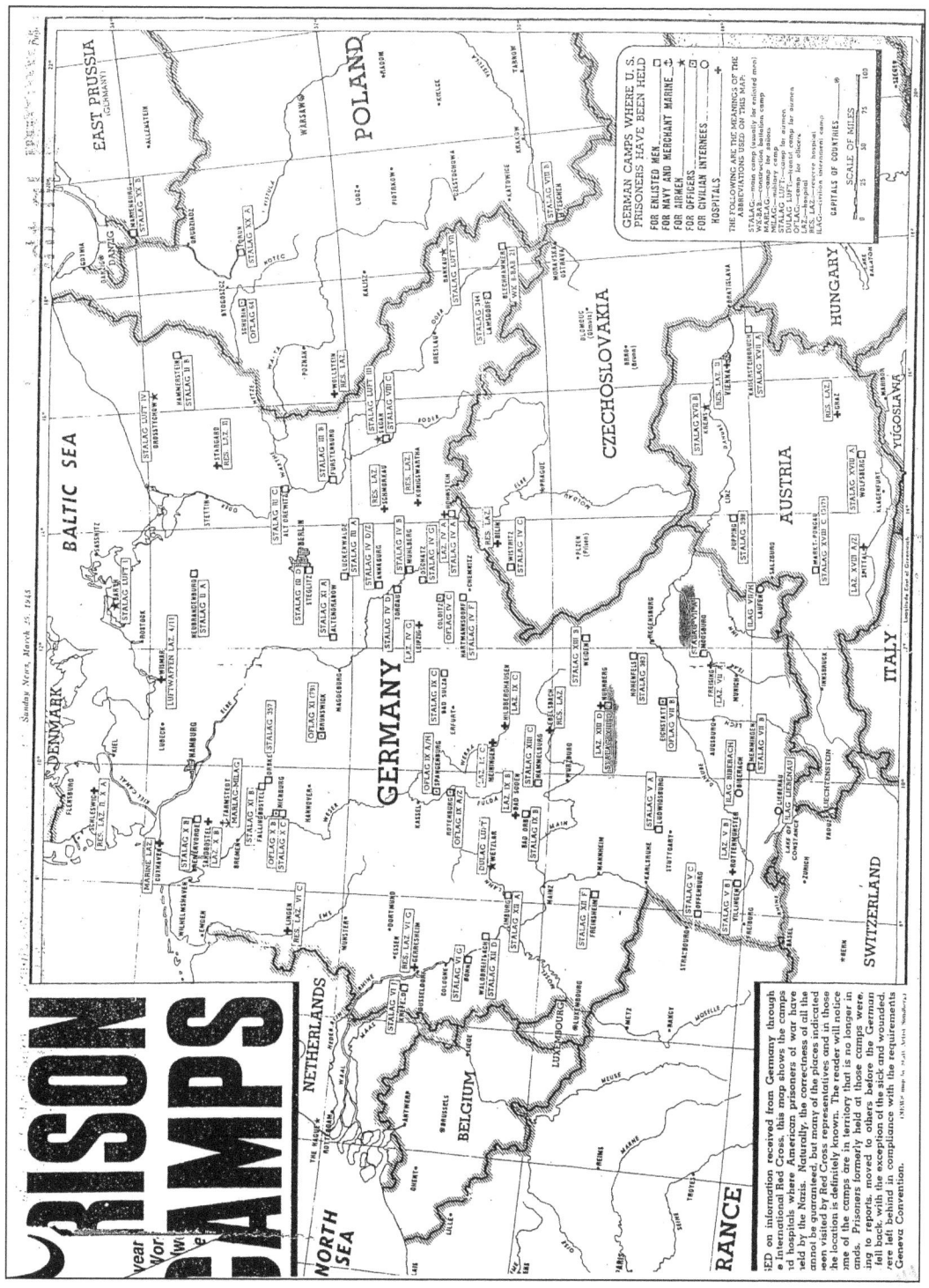

S.S. Prison – Command Head Quarters behind St. Vito's church, Via Roma

Torpedo Factory

Via Roma

Classification **RESTRICTED** CONFIDENTIAL

BRADUNAS, Lt. Col., AC
WRENCH, Capt., AC
1 MAR 1946

MISSING AIR CREW REPORT   13050

1. ORGANIZATION: Location Celone, Italy _____ Command or Air Force 15th Air Force
   Group 463rd Bombardment Group (H) _____ Squadron 772nd Bombardment Sq. (H)
2. SPECIFY: Place of departure Celone, Italy _____ Course As Briefed
   Target Amstettin, Aust _____ Type of mission Att. Aer. Bomb Mission
3. WEATHER CONDITIONS AND VISIBILITY AT TIME OF CRASH OR WHEN LAST REPORTED:
   Weather — Hazy   Visibility — 10 to 15 miles
4. GIVE: [a] Date 20 Mar 1945   Time 1448   Last known position 45°45'N, 14°41'E
   [b] Specify whether: [ ] Last sighted, [ ] Forced down, [ ] Seen to crash,
   [x] Last contacted by radio, [ ] No information.
5. AIRCRAFT ~~WAS~~ [BELIEVED LOST] AS A RESULT OF: [Check one only]
   [ ] Enemy aircraft, [ ] Enemy anti aircraft, [x] Other Pulling excessive power (lost of engines)
6. AIRCRAFT: Type, model & series B-17G _____ AAF Serial Number 44-6377
7. NICKNAME OF AIRCRAFT Pretty Baby's Boys
8. ENGINES: Type, model & series R-1820-97 _____ AAF Serial Number [a] SW-022812
   [b] SW-012512   [c] SW-026400   [d] SW-017973
9. INSTALLED WEAPONS: [Make, type and serial number] MG, Br Acft Basic, M-2, 50 Cal, W/R slides
   [a] 1756226   [e] 1307119   [i] 1306944
   [b] 1755659   [f] 1306523   [j] 1756254
   [c] 1305173   [g] 1307329   [k] 1305963
   [d] 1306250   [h] 1305928   [l] 1306180   (m) 1307086
10. PERSONNEL LISTED BELOW REPORTED AS: [x] Battle Casualty, [ ] Non Battle Casualty.
11. NUMBER OF PERSONS ABOARD AIRCRAFT: Crew 10; Passengers 0; Total 10
    [If more than 12 persons aboard aircraft, use separate sheet]

CREW POSITION	FULL NAME [Last, first, initial] RANK, SERIAL NUMBER	CURRENT STATUS	NEXT OF KIN, RELATIONSHIP AND ADDRESS
[1] Pilot 1st Lt	Lincoln, John W. O 444 725	MIA RTD	Genevieve C. Lincoln (W), 472 W. 10, Claremont, Calif RTD
[2] Co-Pilot 2nd Lt	Millard, Lorin L. O 780 673	MIA RTD	Elva L. Millard (W), Route #2, Alliance, Ohio RTD
[3] Nav F/O	Horn, Harvey S. T 131 675	MIA RTD	Esther Horn (M), 1218 41st St, Brooklyn, N.Y. RTD
[4] Bogg Tier Sgt	Wagoner, Hubert R. 35 901 427	MIA RTD	Dott A. Wagoner (M), R.R. #1, Hillsboro, Ind. RTD
[5] Eng Sgt	Linnane, Edward J. 16 002 112	MIA RTD	Margaret Linnane (M), 1527 N. Leamington Ave, Chicago, Illinois RTD
[6] Radio Sgt	Stover, Herbert C. 34 657 623	MIA RTD	C. Stover (M), 5722 American St, Philadelphia, Pa. RTD
[7] Lt Wst Sgt	Herrick, Oren J. 15 354 193	MIA	Herbert W. Herrick (F), 14203 Glenside Rd, Cleveland, Ohio RTD
[8] Rt Wst S/Sgt	Caldwell, Gilbert R. 39 411 128	MIA	W. Ray Caldwell (F), Box #14, Modena, Utah RTD
[9] Ball Sgt	Michel, Richard 38 598 973	MIA RTD	Daisy T. Michel (M), 109 Buchanan St, Stamps, Ark. RTD
[10] Tail Sgt	Brown, Louis D. 17 134 428	MIA	Frank D. Brown (F), 1033 Bell Pl, Hillsboro, Illinois RTD

12. IDENTIFY BELOW THOSE PERSONS WHO ARE BELIEVED TO HAVE LAST KNOWLEDGE OF AIRCRAFT AND CHECK APPROPRIATE [one only] COLUMN TO INDICATE BASIS FOR SAME:

NAME IN FULL	RANK	SERIAL No.	CONTACTED BY RADIO	LAST SIGHTED	SAW CRASH	FORCED LANDING
[1] Kobylenski, Thaddeus F.	1st Lt	O 821 037	X			
[2] Meverhoff, Robert T.	2nd Lt	O 2 039 182	X			

1st Lt. John W. Lincoln	Mr. Elliott G. Lincoln (father) 472 West 10th Street Claremont, California
2nd Lt. Lorin L. Millard	Mrs. Alva L. Millard (wife) Route 2 Louisville, Ohio
F/O Harvey S. Horn	Mrs. E. Horn (mother) 1318 41st Street Brooklyn, New York
S/Sgt. Gilbert R. Caldwell	Mr. Willie R. Caldwell (father) Post Office Box 14 Modena, Utah
Sgt. Richard Nichol	Mrs. Daisy Nichol (mother) 109 Buchanan Stamps, Arkansas
Sgt. Louis D. Brown	Mrs. Jennie L. Brown (mother) 1053 Bell Place Hillsboro, Illinois
Sgt. Oren J. Herrick	Mr. Herbert W. Herrick (father) 14203 Glenside Road Cleveland, Ohio
Sgt. Hubert R. Wagoner	Mr. Ransom R. Wagoner (father) Route #1 Hillsboro, Indiana
Sgt. Edward J. Linnane	Mr. Edward Linnane (father) 1527 North Leamington Avenue Chicago, Illinois
Sgt. Herbert C. Stover	Mrs. Edith Irene Stover (mother) 636 Irby Avenue Laurens, South Carolina

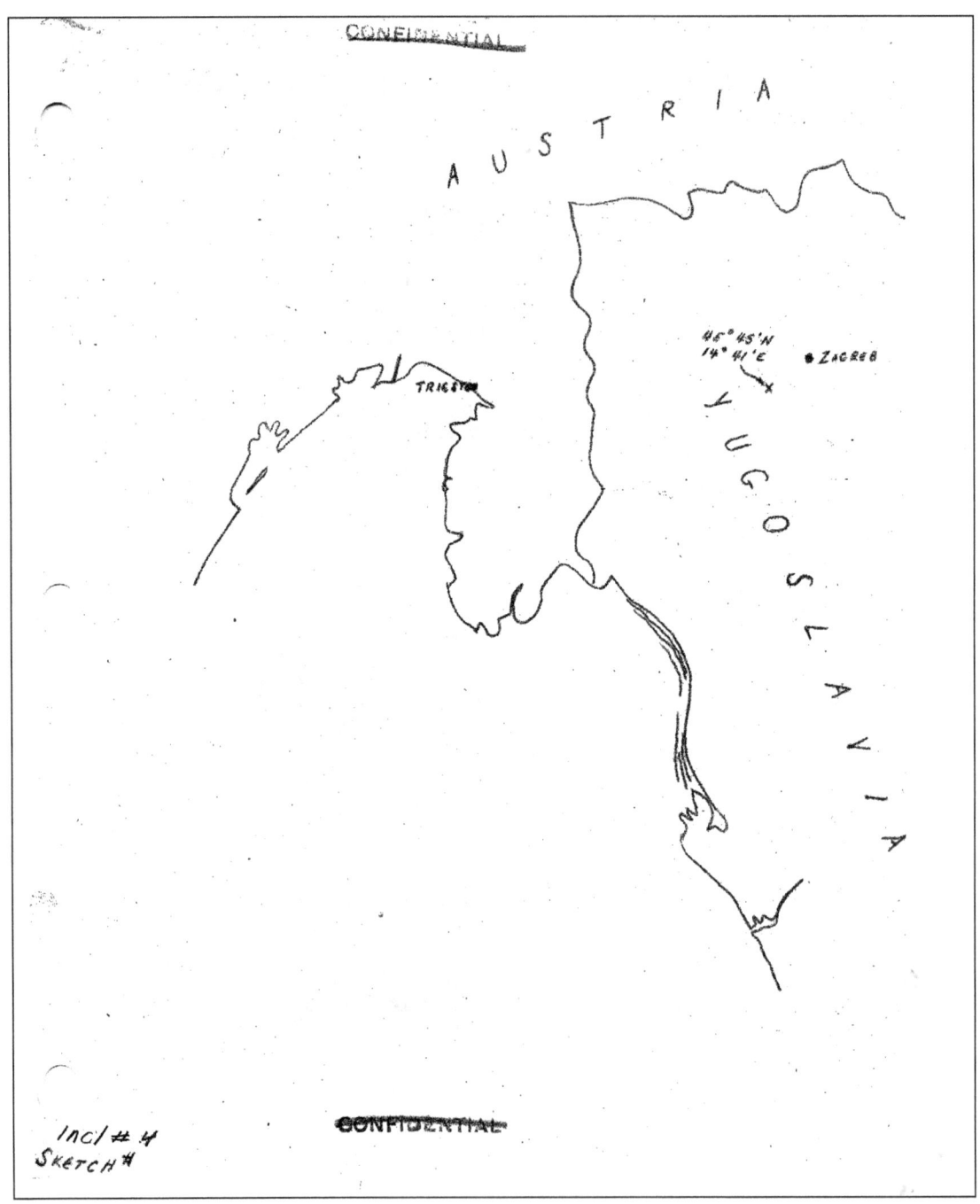

```
FORM LEAF #1                              Restricted
                    STATEMENT ON CAPTURE OR RECOVERY OF MEMBERS OF ENEMY AIR FORCES
REPORT IS MADE THROUGH:                   DISTRIBUTOR:   Flight Command Verona
                                                         Draft
OFFICE OR STATION:    Airbase HQ E (v) 213/VII

LOCATION:  Basaldella/Udine on 27 March 45     OFFICE OR APPRAISAL-VALUES:
```

	DOWNED	)	Super-		
REGARDING:	EMERGENCY LANDINGS)		Fortress	DATE AND TIME:	20 March 45, 1515
	CRASH	)			

(presumably by earlier antiaircraft hits, sunk
20 minutes afer crash)

AT: Gulf of Fiume NEAR:

```
                    PERSONAL RECORD OF MEMBERS OF ENEMY AIR FORCES

              SURNAME    )       HORN              Year of birth: 1923
FAMILY NAME:  LAST NAME  )

              CHRISTIAN NAME)    Harvey Stanley    Last residence before war:
FIRST NAME:   GIVEN NAME  )                        L. Horn
                                                   1218 41th Street
                                                   Brooklyn/New York

RANK:         Flying officer
                              SERIAL
IDENTIFICATION NUMBER:        SERVICE    T-131675

NATIONALITY:
```

STATEMENTS MADE AT TIME OF CAPTURE: /later STATEMENT MADE AT RECOVERY OF DEAD:
DATE OF CAPTURE: 20 March 45, about 1 hour   DATE & TIME & PLACE OF RECOVERY:
EXACT LOCATION OF CAPTURE: same place   CONDITION OF BODY:
CAPTURE EFFECTED BY: Harbor HQ Fiume (crew was drifting in rubber boats)

THE PRISONER WORE (UNIFORM)   DESCRIPTION OF IDENTIFICATION TAG:
                                         HOW WERE PERSONAL RECORDS OF DEAD
                                         ASCERTAINED?

                                         DATE AND TIME OF BURIAL:
                                         GRAVE LOCATION:

POSSIBLE IMPUTATION (PLACING) UNDER SERVICE OF THE
G.F.P. OR S.D., FOR PURPOSE OF ASCERTAINING ENEMY
PATRONAGE OR FAVOR:

DELIVERED TO HOSPITAL:
DATE:

DATE AND TIME OF TRANSPORTATION TO
PRISONER CONCENTRATION POINT:

REMARKS: all crew members have been rescued and captured.

(ATTEMPTED ESCAPE. PECULIARITIES IN BEHAVIOR OF PRISONER, ETC.)   signed: Granier
INVENTORY OF SECURED, PERSONAL EFFECTS OF PRISONER OR DEAD: Colonel and Commander
INVENTORY OF PERSONAL EFFECTS AND EQUIPMENT OF PRISONER OR DEAD:
                                                                 6-3224.AF(3)

~~CONFIDENTIAL~~

772ND BOMBARDMENT SQUADRON (H)
463RD BOMBARDMENT GROUP (H)
APO   520

21 MARCH 1945.

STATEMENT

SHIP #44-6377, MISSING IN ACTION 20 MARCH 1945.

SHIP #44-6377 WAS FLYING LOW UNDER OUR GROUP AFTER LOOSING ONE ENGINE, TURBO OUT ON ANOTHER, OIL LEAK ON THE OTHER. HE CALLED UP EASY LEADER AND TOLD HIS TROUBLES AND WOULD PROBABLEY BAIL OUT DUE TO THE HIGH TERRAIN BEFORE HIM. I BELIEVE IT WAS NUMBER TWO ENGINE THAT WENT OUT NEXT AND THEN NUMBER THREE WAS SMOKING AND THAT ALSO WENT OUT. DOG LEADER ALSO TALKED TO EASY LEADER AND CALLED UP SHIP #377. SHIP #377 WAS TOLD HE WAS 60 MILES AWAY FROM THE COAST SO TO TRY AND MAKE IT AND DITCH. HE SEEMED TO BE DOING EVERYTHING POSSIBLE TO LIGHTEN THE LOAD AND THREW EVERYTHING OVERBOARD. THE COAST WAS IN SIGHT BUT CONTACT WAS NOT MADE WITH SHIP #377. EASY LEADER TURNED THE LEAD OVER TO EASY TWO AND CIRCLED THE AREA TO OBSERVE SHIP #377. ALSO A P-38 WAS IN THE VICINITY. ALL CONVERSATION HEARD ON "B" CHANNEL, VHF.

Thaddeus F. Kobylenski
THADDEUS F. KOBYLENSKI,
1ST LT, AIR CORPS,
PILOT, EASY TWO.

~~CONFIDENTIAL~~

C-O-N-F-I-D-E-N-T-I-A-L

772ND BOMBARDMENT SQUADRON (H)
463RD BOMBARDMENT GROUP (H)
APO 520

21 MARCH 1945.

S-T-A-T-E-M-E-N-T

SHIP #44-6377, MISSING IN ACTION 20 MARCH 1945.

SHIP #44-6377, CALLED EASY LEADER ON WAY TO PRIMARY TARGET TELLING HIM THAT HE HAD ONE ENGINE OUT DUE TO PULLING EXCESSIVE POWER, ALSO JETTISIONED BOMBS TO KEEP UP. AFTER BOMBS AWAY ON FIRST ALTERNATE, HE HAD TWO PROPS FEATHERED AND ONE TURBO OUT ON ONE OF THE REMAINING ENGINES. CALLED EASY LEADER AND TOLD HIM HE WAS LOOSING 700 FEET PER MIN, I.A.S. 150 MPH. HE REQUESTED PERMISSION TO BAIL OUT, PERMISSION REFUSED BY DOG LEADER. ADVICE FROM DOG LEADER; JETTISION GUNS, AMMO, AND TURRETS. TRIED TO CATCH FORMATION. 60 MIDES FROM COAST, SHIP #377 CALLED DOG LEADER AND TOLD HIM HE WOULD TRY TO MAKE COAST AND DITCH. LAST HEARD FROM OVER ALPS IN NORTHERN YUGO STATING THAT HE WOULD HEAD DOWN THE COAST. P-38 AND EASY ONE UNABLE TO LOCATE SHIP #377.

Robert T. Meyerhoff
ROBERT T. MEYERHOFF,
2ND LT, AIR CORPS,
PILOT, EASY THREE.

C-O-N-F-I-D-E-N-T-I-A-L

```
                    C-O-N-F-I-D-E-N-T-I-A-L
                 772ND BOMBARDMENT SQUADRON (H)
                  463RD BOMBARDMENT GROUP (H)
                       APO        520
```

21 MARCH 1945.

S-T-A-T-E-M-E-N-T

SHIP #44-6377, MISSING IN ACTION 20 MARCH 1945.

WHILE RETURNING FROM THE TARGET, SHIP #44-6377, HAD FEATHERED TWO ENGINES AND WAS FLYING IN DOG SQUADRON. THE FORMATION SLOWED UP SO SHIP #~~33~~-6377 COULD STAY WITH US. JUST BEFORE REACHING THE COAST, ANOTHER ENGINE STARTED SMOKING ON SHIP #377. HE LEFT THE FORMATION AND WAS LOOSING ALTITUDE RAPIDLY. I LAST SAW SHIP #377 BREAKING TO THE RIGHT UNDER THE FORMATION. THE PILOT, LT LINCOLN, SAID HE THOUGHT HE COULD CLEAR THE MOUNTAINS AHEAD AND REACH THE COAST. WE LEFT THE SQUADRON AND PATROLLED THE AREA TRYING TO FIND SHIP #377. WE ALSO PATROLLED THE COAST THINKING HE MAY HAVE DITCHED. WE COULD NOT CONTACT SHIP #377 ON VHF OR SPOT HIS SHIP. I DO NOT BELIEVE HE REACHED THE COAST TO DITCH.

Venanzio Del Signore
VENANZIO DEL SIGNORE,
1ST LT, AIR CORPS,
PILOT, EASY ONE.

```
                    C-O-N-F-I-D-E-N-T-I-A-L
```

LOCATION	ORGANIZATION		RECIPIENT	NEXT DESTINATION	CRATED OR FLY-AWAY	CONDITION	DATE 1944		ACTION		REMARKS
	OWNER	PARENT UNIT	SUB UNIT	GAINED FROM OR LOST TO		SERIAL NUMBER	MO	DA	STATION NO	OK A	
Long Beach	Douglas					Accepted	7-20				
"	"		Bosley Proj Section C/ Hunter Fld, Ga		F	Available	7-18	7-1585			CET Whitfore 1-LR+ 675 gal
"			"	"	18	Delivered	7-20		JFR		
Cincinnati		ATC	"	"	3	departed	7-21		"		
"		"	"	"	42	enroute del	7-22		"		
Hunter Fld		"	"	"	73	arrived	7-22		saw A&R 3		
"		"	N Atlantic Wing/Dom			departed	7-29				
						arriv.	8-1				
						dp H.S.	8-3		FM		
PRESQUE	ATC		NA	ENROUT POUS A3		B17 644	6377	8 6	1279	6 9	8783
OHAN	15 A			A B17G	12	44	6377	8	344		
OHAN	15 A			C B17G	10 44		6377	8	344		
FOGGIA	CON		MIA	R B17G L 12	44		6377		32045	1144	

MAY BE SAFE

Sgt. Dwain Brown, son of Mr. nd Mrs. Frank D. Brown of Hillsboro, who was reported missing several weeks ago following a light over Yugoslavia, is believed afe and his parents expect to hear om him soon.

Relatives of the pilot, co-pilot nd navigator on the plane on which Sgt. Brown was tail gunner, have been freed and have ontacted relatives in this country aying they were fine. In their essa— home they said the other (of the plane crew were .n the three officers say re_ .t about April 1.

Relatives of the officers sent is information to Mr. and Mrs. rown here, who hope to hear on that their son is free and safe.

Missing in Action

Sgt. Louis Dwaine Brown of Hillsboro is reported as missing in action in recent combat as a gunner on a B-17 bombing plane over Yugoslavia. His parents, Mr and Mrs. Frank D. Brown of Hillsboro received a message yesterday from the War Department stating he had been missing since March 20.

DWAINE BROW IS MISSING I AERIAL COMBA

Hillsboro Youth W: in Action Over Yugoslavia

Sgt. Louis Dwaine Brown Hillsboro is reported as missi in action over Yugoslavia Mar 20 according to a message recei ed yesterday by his parents, M and Mrs. Frank D. Brown of th city. The message from the W: Department stated that the pa ents would be notified as promp ly as further news was obtaine

Sgt. Brown went into the ser ice on December 16, 1943, wit Cpl. Harold Brown, son of Att and Mrs. McLin Brown of Hill boro. Cpl. Harold Brown has r cently been reported missing action and is believed to hav met death in softening up the a tack on Japan on a bomber plan However, the two Hillsboro avi tors had not been together for long time. They both went to F Sheridan for basic training an then together to Gulfport, Miss where they were together for time until Sgt. Dawine Brown wer to Jefferson Barracks and then t Kearns, Utah, Los Vagas, Nev., t a gunnery school, then to Tampa Fla. and later to Savannah, Ga after which he went oversee about January 22 this year an was believed to be based in South ern Italy. He was a gunner o a B-17 bomber plane.

Sgt. Brown was born and rear ed in Hillsboro being a son of Mr and Mrs. Frank D. Brown, she be ing the former Jennie Stivers o Nokomis. He has a brother, Or ville Brown, who is a student i the Hillsboro Community Hig school. His grandparents, Mr and Mrs. Robert G. Brown reside in Hillsboro and his materna grandmother, Mrs. R. L. Stiver lives in Witt. He was 19 on No vember 25, 1944.

Sgt. Dwaine Brown graduated a the Hillsboro Community Hig school in May 1943 and enlisted immediately but was not calle until December 16. He is an am bitious young man and a hard and efficient worker as he demonstart ed through the fact that he had some kind of a job from the time he was old enough to accept i and was last employed at the Sey mour Drug store here. His host of relatives and friends in the com munity are hoping for early re ports from the War Departmen giving good news of his havi been located.

THREE HILLSBORO MEN MEET

A field press censored report from the 15th AAF in Italy says: "From Hillsboro, did you say? well, so are we."

Thus met three men from Hillsboro, recently assigned to the same 15th AAF B-17 Flying Fortress squadron in Italy. The three men are from different states. however. Posed before a pile of wrecked German JU-88s the men are, left to right: Cpl. Donald E. Charles B. Sprinkle, Route 2, Hillsboro, Ohio; Cpl. Hubert R. Wagoner, 20, son of Mr. and Mrs. Ranson Wagoner, Hillsboro, Indiana, and Cpl. Louis Dwain Brown, 19, son of Mr. and Mrs. Frank D. Brown, 1033 Bell Place, Hillsboro, Illinois. Sprinkle is an engineer-gunner, Wagoner an enlisted bombardier and Brown a tail gunner. The latter two are on the same crew, having met

holding of a general power of attorney can not be deemed an authorization for any such new ventures. Requests for new allotments should be made and the necessity established by dependents or others concerned, requests being for whatever may be actually necessary but no more. Particular attention of relatives of absentees is called to making certain that commercial or governmental life insurance premiums continue to be paid by allotment or otherwise.

CHANGES IN FAMILY ALLOWANCES

During an enlisted man's absence in any casualty status family allowances in effect at the beginning of absence may be changed just as though he continued on a duty status. This means increases or decreases due to births, deaths, marriages of children, or attainment by children of limiting age, any of which effect a change in the family group. There may be decreases or increases due to degree of dependency changing from that for chief support to that for only substantial portion of support or the reverse. _____ may be changes also incident to divorce or court orders affecting maintenance. It is expected _____ and prompt reports of any such changes, including copies of records

Revised 15 March 1945.

harvey

From: "Danijel Frka" <danijel.frka@ri.t-com.hr>
To: <harmini@optonline.net>; "Danijel Frka" <frka@rij...
Sent: Monday, March 19, 2007 1:42 PM
Subject: Re:Pretty baby's Boys

Dear Harvey,
Finally I managed to contact Mr. Ivo Simonic. He told me the same story as already written by Denis Romac, and as he was at the age of 12 at that time he does not remember much more. I shall try to reproduce his story the best way I could.
Well, as we know he was a 12-year old boy and he was living in a house on the slope above the city center. He remembers that there was a beautiful winter day in March 1945. and he was sitting on a small square with a group of other children. As they were used to false air raid warnings which happened many times a day, he didn't pay attention to these sounds any more. Suddenly a roar of aircraft engines shook them all up and amazed they looked to the sky. The next instant a big four engined bomber suddenly appeared directly over them coming from the north, very low and heading out to the open sea. The aircraft was very low and they could all see the star and bars under the wing. It was clear that the plane was in trouble as it has been trailing a thin smoke behind. They rushed to the end of the square from where they could see the direction in which tha crippled plane was flying. There, leaned to the stone fence were two German SS officers who were also observing the plane. Although the war was almost over, they were still in perfectly ironed uniforms with polished boots, and they were observing the plane with field binoculars. The plane went lower and lower until it ditched a few miles off the port of Rijeka, roughly in the middle of the Kvarner bay. One of the two officers lowered his binoculars, turned to the other one and said in German (which Mr. Simonic speaks fluently so he could understand): "Those must be damned good pilots, able to ditch perfectly such a plane!" About an hour or less later, they all observed a small patrol craft leaving Rijeka harbour and heading for the spot where the plane ditched.
Next day Mr. Simonic heard that the Germans rescued 9 American airmen, and that some of them were black. But he knew that these were only half-informations.
Regarding the whereabouts of the building where you were taken in, he does not know anything.
So this is what I recorded from Mr. Simonic's story. Unfortunately I forgot to ask him if he speaks English but I shall call him again.
We will keep looking fot other eye-witnesses.

With best regards,
Danijel Frka

>
> Subject:
> Pretty baby's Boys
> From:
> "harvey" <harmini@optonline.net>
> Date:
> Sun, 18 Mar 2007 23:45:14 +0100
> To:
> "Danijel Frka" <frka@rijekapromet.hr>
>
> To:
> "Danijel Frka" <frka@rijekapromet.hr>
>
>
> Danijel,
> The markings on the tail of Perty Baby's Boys show a black circle
> background with a *white Y *in the center. If you go to www.463rd.com
> <http://www.463rd.com> you will pick up our website.

NOVA LIST FEBRUARY 26, 2007

RIJEKA - American citizen, Harvey Horn, needed almost 62 years to close a chapter in his life during Worl War II. Harvey, as a naviagtor on a B17 Bomber, was shot down by the Germans a month and a half before the end of the war - to be exact on March 20, 1945. Horn and 9 other flyers fell into the Adriatic sea. They were quickly picked up by a German patrol boat and transported to Rijeka. Today after 62 plus years, Horn is back in Rijeka but now as a tourist and a friend of the people of Rijeka and welcomed with open arms.

Harvey Horn, assigned to Bomber Group 463rd, Bomber Squadron 772 was based in Italy. His plane left the city of Foggia to go towards Austria to a city called Amsttetin near Vienna. They were flying over 30,000 feet high over the Adriatic Sea near the Yugoslavian border. Before they reached their destination, their plane, which they called "Pretty Baby's Boys" was shot by the Germans. The plane has four engines but the Germans hit two of them leaving the plane with only two engines running. The plane was losing altitude and they decided to drop all their fighting cargo and try to return to their base in Italy. While losing altitude and speed, the Germans hit them again and before they knew it, Horn and his crew found themselves in the Adriatic Sea.

Horn pointed to the approximate place where the plane went down. After the plane went down, Horn and the crew took a raft and started paddling to shore. Before they knew it, a German patrol boat found them at sea. Horn said they knew they were Germans and that he and crew would be prisoners of war. The Germans took their guns and whatever else they had and the German patrol boat followed them back to shore. When they arrived in Rijeka at sundown, many people from Rijeka came to see the the Americans pilots as prisoners of war. Horn felt as a if he was a caged animal on exhibition through the streets of Rijeka with all eyes staring at them. They were taken behind one of the buildings and lined up against a wall with machine guns pointed at them. Horn remembers thinking that they were going to get shot. Horn remembers that wall very well.

After some time, they were taken into the building and put in a room where they stayed one night as prisoners in Rijeka. They were tired, wet and very weak. Horn said they were given some kind of black bread and some funny kind of black coffee that night and in the morning, which didn't agree with Mr Horn who had to run to the bathroom every so often. After breakfast, they were taken to the center of Rijeka by trolley where they were mixed with civilians. The Germans were all over the place. I was 21 years old and in a trolley next to me on one side there was an extremely beautiful looking girl. On the other side, a German soldier. Even today, I remember that beautiful looking girl.

Later that morning, Horn and his crew left the train station in Rijeka to go to Trieste. They spent a few days in Trieste before going to northern Italy and ultimately Germany. During his stay in Trieste, which was about 4 or five days, the worst thing that happened to them was the lack of food. You know, I am a jew and I never thought that I would find myself in that kind of a situation, a prisoner of war in German hands. You can imagine how I felt. Did Horn know about Hitler's concentration camps for Jews and other European people he didn't like. Very little, almost nothing. He was born in Brooklyn, New York and today lives in Monroe in the State of New York. He volunteered for the American Army because he thought it was the right thing to do because America was attacked. He was an engineer. He loved to fly and loved planes.

When Horn and his crew reached Munich, the crew was separated. The enlisted men were sent to Mooseburg and Horn and his pilot and copilot were sent to Nuremburg. Under the seige of Nuremburg, Horn and 18 others were marched out. That night Horn collapsed on the road. The Germans were going shoot but someone convinced the guards to surrender as the war was almost over. After hiding in a barn that night, they met the American Army the next morning. A German Officer tried to talk Horn and the others into fighting the Russians because the Germans were afraid of Russians and Communism.

After all he went through, Horn never spoke about his ordeal to anybody and he never took advantage of the benefits provided to war veterns with the exception of the GI Bill to return to college. Only in recent years has Horn started to talk about his experiences. There must be a better was to solve problems than war. It is the option of last resort.

BOX/ Horn wanted to go back to Rijeka but it was only a dream until he met Wanda S Radetti, born in Rijeka. She is a travel agent specializing in Croatia. She is the economic and cultural agent for Rijeka in America. Her parents were born in Rijeka and after World War II her parents left Rijeka. Wanda said she loves the people who love freedom and that is what Harvey S Horn is doing with a smile on his face after the bad experience of war.

April 26 1945

D.

Dear Family

I am in Amerix a hands. Was a prisoner for awhile. OK using a german typwriter will tell you all the stuff when i get home which should be soon.
The whole crew is ok too. I hope you haven(t worried too much. Things in Germany are bad and the war will be over soon so the Red Cross has a job getting reports home to the families back home on PW.

Hope to leave Germany tonight foHoFrance and then England. listening to musicwhich is wonderful and eating.

We took 23 Germans when the Americans finally caught us and they had 19 American officers freed.

See you soon

All my Love
Harvey

WESTERN UNION CABLEGRAM

1945 MAY 8 AM 11 51

N49 INTL=CD SANS ORIGINE VIA RCA
EFM MRS E HORN=
1218 41 ST BROOKLYN NY=

ALL WELL AND SAFE. HOPE TO SEE YOU SOON. ALL MY LOVE=
HARVEY S HORN.

WESTERN UNION CABLEGRAM

1945 MAY 27 PM 12 33

N30 INTL=CD SANS ORIGINE (VIA RCA)
EFM MRS E HORN=
1218 41 ST BROOKLYN NY 18=

ALL WELL AND SAFE. HOPE TO SEE YOU SOON ALL MY LOVE=
HARVEY HORN.

```
                FIFTEENTH AIR FORCE
         Office of the Commanding General
                   A. P. O. 520
```

31 May 1945

Mrs. Esther Horn
1218 41st Street
Brooklyn 18, New York

My dear Mrs. Horn:

Your recent letter of inquiry regarding your son, Flight Officer Harvey Horn, T-131675, who was reported missing in action on March 20, 1945, has been received.

All postal money order records for this air force are forwarded to the Postmaster, New York City, New York. It is suggested that you send all the available information regarding your son's money order to his office for action.

I regret that we have had no further news of Harvey at this headquarters since our letter of April 3, 1945. With the cessation of hostilities in Europe every effort is being made to locate men who are still carried as missing in action. It is my earnest hope that definite word of your son's fate will be forthcoming in the near future.

Very sincerely yours,

JAMES A. MOLLISON
Brigadier General, USA
Commanding

CERTIFICATE IN LIEU OF LOST OR DESTROYED

Certificate of Service

This is to certify that

HARVEY S HORN T 131 675 Flight Officer AC

honorably served in active Federal Service in the Army of the United States from 26 August 1944 *to* 11 August 1945

Given at the War Department, Washington, D.C., on

21 July 1948

By order of the Secretary of War:

Ernest E. Johnson
Adjutant General

ARMY SEPARATION QUALIFICATION RECORD

ARMY SEPARATION CENTER, FORT DIX, N.J.

THIS FORM WILL NOT BE REPLACED IF LOST OR DESTROYED. SAVE IT.

LAST NAME – FIRST NAME – MIDDLE INITIAL	ARMY SERIAL NUMBER	GRADE	DATE OF ENTRY INTO ACTIVE SERVICE	SEX	DATE OF BIRTH
HORN HARVEY S	T-131 675	F/O	26 Aug 44	M	15 Dec 23

PERMANENT ADDRESS FOR MAILING PURPOSES (Street and Number - City - County - State): 82-15 Britton Ave., Elmhurst, Queens County, New York

CIVILIAN EDUCATION

HIGHEST GRADE COMPLETED	LAST YEAR OF ATTENDANCE	HIGHEST DEGREE RECEIVED	MAJOR COURSE OF STUDY	NAME AND ADDRESS OF LAST SCHOOL ATTENDED
1½ yrs. College	1943	NONE	Mech. Eng.	Pratt Institute, Brooklyn, New York

OTHER TRAINING OR SCHOOLING: NONE

SERVICE EDUCATION

SERVICE SCHOOL	COURSE	WKS. OR HRS.	RATING	ARMY SPECIALIZED TRAINING PROGRAM — INSTITUTION WHERE ENROLLED	CURRICULUM AND TERM (COURSE OF TRAINING PURSUED)	NO. OF WEEKS	GRADUATED YES/NO
Army Air Forces Schools	Avn. Cadet Pilot Tng.	14	Comp	U. of Vermont	College Tng. Detachment	14	Comp
	Flexible Gunnery	6	"		Called to Cadet Tng. prior to completion of course.		Not
	Adv. Navigation	20	"				

CIVILIAN OCCUPATIONS

MAIN OCCUPATION (TITLE): STUDENT, COLLEGE
SECONDARY OCCUPATION (TITLE): NONE

MILITARY SPECIALTIES

YEARS	MONTHS	GRADE	PRINCIPAL DUTY	ARMY CODE NO.	YEARS	MONTHS	GRADE	PRINCIPAL DUTY	ARMY CODE NO.
1	0	F/O	Navigator	1034					

SUMMARY OF MILITARY OCCUPATION AND CIVILIAN CONVERSIONS (Shown by title)

NAVIGATOR: Served as Navigator on B-17 with 463rd Bombardment Group, 15th Air Force on bombing missions over enemy-occupied Europe. Shot down over Fiume. Prisoner of War 5 weeks. Trained as Navigator in Pan-American School. Holds certificate qualifying as Commercial Navigator.

DECORATIONS: European Theatre Ribbon with 2 Battle Stars.
Enlisted Service: Basic Tng. Mar. to Apr. 1943. Aviation Cadet Tng. Apr 43 to Aug. 44.

THIS INFORMATION BASED ON SOLDIER'S STATEMENT. (Indicate by * any items not supported by military records)

DATE OF SEPARATION: 11 Aug 45
SIGNATURE OF SOLDIER: *Harvey S Horn*
SIGNATURE OF SEPARATION CLASSIFICATION OFFICER: *W. W. Von Schlichten*
W.W. VON SCHLICHTEN, MAJ. AGD

I.D., A.G.O. FORM NO. 100   15 July 1944

_____ (Date)

SUBJECT: Pass for Paris Area

TO : Whom It May Concern

_____
(Name)   (Rank)   (ASN)   (Organization)

The above named person has just returned from a "Missing in Action" status, and is authorized to be in the Paris area. He is billeted at the Hotel Francia, 100 Rue Lafayette, Paris, (PW & X Det, Office of the Director of Intelligence, Hq, US Strategic Air Forces in Europe). He will not be able to comply with existing uniform regulations due to his recent return to duty.

For the Commanding General:

R. E. FECTEAU
Captain, AGD
Asst Adj General

C O N F I D E N T I A L
(Equals British Secret)

Headquarters
European Theater of Operations
P/W and X Detachment
Military Intelligence Service

5 May 1945
(Date)

The following named officer/EM has been missing in action and proper identification papers are being prepared. He is in London for official purposes and is unable to conform with existing uniform regulations.

F/O Harvy S Horn T-131675

For the Commanding Officer:

JOHN F WHITE, JR
Captain, AC
63 Brook Street
Regent 8484, ext 2596

C O N F I D E N T I A L
(Equals British Secret)

AUTHORIZATION FOR ALLOTMENT OF PAY
(See AR 35-5520)

HORN HARVEY S 12176169 PVT SQ B-70
(Last name) (First name) (Middle initial) (Army serial No.) (Grade) (Company, regiment, or arm or service)

The *officer/*enlisted man named above hereby authorizes a Class E allotment of his pay in the amount of $ 6.50 Adv. ded. for mo. of MAR 1943 per month for the period of _____ months, commencing MARCH 19, 1943, and expiring E.T.S. 19__

to Director of Insurance, Veterans Administration, Washington, D.C.
(Name of allottee) (Number and street or rural route) (City, town, or post office) (State)

Date of enlistment MARCH 18, 1943. When other than "Pay of the Army" is affected, state P. A. chargeable //

I hereby state that the purpose for which this allotment is granted is solely for the support of wife, child, or dependent relatives; or if made for the payment of life insurance premiums, the insurance (including endowments and/or twenty (or other) payment policies) is on the life of the allotter only; that a policy therefor has been issued and the first premium paid thereon; that the insurance constitutes the major and not a merely incidental or collateral element of the transaction; and that the allotment is made in favor of the insurance company issuing the policy and not in favor of a bank or other agent. I also state if allotment is in favor of a bank that deposit should be made to the credit of

//
(Name) (Relationship)

Harvey S Horn
(Signature of allotter)

Send directly to Finance Officer, U.S. Army, Washington, D.C.

PRTD (Prov) AAFTTC, Atlantic City, N.J.
Date March 19, 1943

Entered on service record 3/20 1943

W.D., A.G.O. Form No. 29
October 11, 1941
*Strike out words not applicable
(Signature of commanding officer or personnel officer, with grade and organization)
Assistant Personnel Officer

CONFIDENTIAL

CERTIFIED THAT:

No. _____ Grade 2L OFF NAME (Full) HARVEY S. HORN
CLAIMS ASSIGNMENT TO FOLLOWING UNIT Hq & 6 772 B SQD

Security reasons do/do not exist preventing his return to combat duty.

He was a PW/_____ for a period of 34 days.

Individual has/_____ been identified.

Steve Cunningham
Capt, Col.

IMPORTANT: THIS CERTIFICATE MUST BE RETAINED AND HANDED TO (BRITISH) AN OFFICER OF MI9 OR (AMERICAN) AN OFFICER OF MIS-X ON ARRIVAL IN U.K. OR U.S.A.

CONFIDENTIAL

HEADQUARTERS
NINTH AIR FORCE
ADVANCED

APO 696, U. S. Army
29 April 1945

SUBJECT: Travel Orders.

TO: 1ST LT JOHN H. COMBS, 0742085, AC.   F/O HARVEY S. HORN, T131675,
    1ST LT JOHN W. LINCOLN, 0444725, AC.   F/O MIKE REAGAN, T127981, AC
    2D LT LEONARD M. JANES, 01683582, AC.
    2D LT WILLIAM H. SCHUMI, 02075316, AC.
    2D LT LORIN L. MILLARD, 0780673, AC.

1. You will proceed on or about 29 April 1945 from this Hq to Paris, France, reporting upon arrival thereat to Interrogation officer, Francia Hotel for the purpose of being returned to proper organization and station through PW channels

XXXXXXXXXXXXXXXXXXXXXXXXXXXXXXXXXXXXXXXXXXXXXXXXXXXXXXXXXXXXXXXXXXXXXXXXXXXXX
XXXXXXXXXXXXXXXXXXXXXXXXXXXX

2. Travel by motor transport, military or commercial aircraft (Par 3b, AR 55-120, 26 April 1943) or rail is authorized. Motor transportation at each station and to the next station visited will be furnished by each station for this temporary duty. TDN pursuant to the authority contained in Ltr, Hq, European TO USA, 22 Nov 1944, file 300.4 PM: 60-114 P 432-02 A 212/50425.

By command of Lieutenant General VANDENBERG:

W W MILLARD
Col G S C
C of S

OFFICIAL:

HARRY E KOCH
Major A G D
Asst Adj Gen

DISTRIBUTION:

2 cys ea Off concerned
1 cy Dir of Int
1 cy AG Files

R E S T R I C T E D

HEADQUARTERS
ARMY AIR FORCES CENTRAL FLYING TRAINING COMMAND
Office of the Commanding General

Randolph Field, Texas

In reply
refer to: AG 201   Horn, Harvey Stanley

Subject: Appointment as Flight Officer.

To: Aviation Cadet Harvey Stanley Horn,
       U.S.A.,   A   T-131,675
       Coral Gables, Fla.

    1. Under authority granted by the Secretary of War, you are appointed a Flight Officer, Army of the United States to rank from this date. Your serial number is shown after A above.

    2. This appointment will continue in force for the duration of the war and six months thereafter unless sooner terminated.

    3. There is inclosed herewith a form for oath of office which you are requested to execute and return. The execution and return of the required oath of office constitute an acceptance of your appointment. No other evidence of acceptance is required.

    4. This letter should be retained by you as evidence of your appointment.

    By command of Brigadier General KRAUS:

J. E. McCORD
Lt. Colonel, A.G.D.
Assistant Adjutant General

Inclosure:
  Form for oath of office.

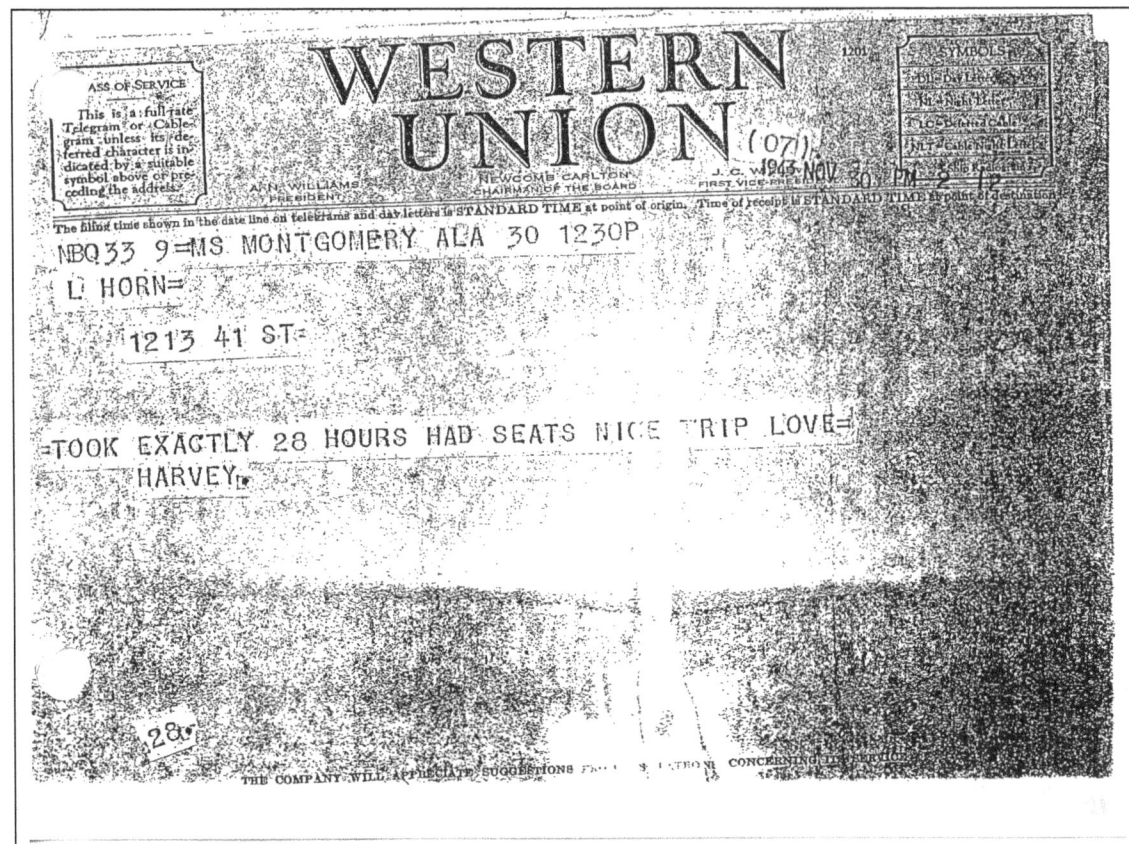

ENLISTED RECORD OF

Horn, Harvey S., 12176169, Avn/Cadet
(Last name) (First name) (Middle initial) (Army serial number) (Grade)

Born in Brooklyn in the State of New York
Enlisted 30 October, 1942 at 480 Lexington Ave., New York City, N.Y.
When enlisted he was 18 10/12 years of age and by occupation a Student.
He had Brown eyes, Brown hair, fair complexion,
and was 5 feet 8 inches in height.
Completed 1 years, 9 months, 27 days service for longevity pay.
Prior service: None

MIAMI AIR DEPOT FLA
F.S PAID IN FULL $125.
25 AUGUST 1944
W TROOLIN MAJ FD
DEPUTY

Noncommissioned officer: Never
Military qualifications: None
Army specialty: Aerial Gunner-15 Apr 44-F/M, Fla.
Attendance at: 2551st AAFBU (CNS) Coral Gables, Fla.
(Name of noncommissioned officers' or special service school)

Battles, engagements, skirmishes, expeditions: none
Decorations, service medals, citations: none
Wounds received in service: none
Date and result of smallpox vaccination: 7-29-44
Date of completion of all typhoid-paratyphoid vaccinations: 4-15-44 Stim. Blood Type A.
Date and result of diphtheria immunity test (Schick): None
Date of other vaccinations (specify vaccine used): Stim. Tet. 7-29-44.
Physical condition when discharged: good   Married or single: single
Honorably discharged by reason of: CofG, par. 25, AR 615-160 to accept appointment AUS
Character: Excellent AFB   Periods of active duty: none
Remarks: No time lost under AW 107

FOR CONVENIENCE, A CERTIFICATE OF ELIGIBILITY No. 1875839 HAS BEEN
ISSUED BY THE VETERANS ADMINISTRATION TO BE USED FOR THE FUTURE REQUEST
OF ANY GUARANTY OR INSURANCE BENEFIT UNDER TITLE III OF THE SERVICEMEN'S
READJUSTMENT ACT OF 1944, IS ADVISED— THAT MAY BE AVAILABLE
PERSON TO WHOM THIS CERTIFICATE IS ISSUED.

Signature of soldier: Harvey S. Horn

JESSE H. BROWN
Major, Air Corps
Commanding 2551st AAF Base Unit

Print of Right Thumb

INSTRUCTIONS FOR ENLISTED RECORD

1 Enter date of induction only in case of trainee inducted under Selective Training and Service Act of 1940 (Bull. 25, W. D., 1940); in all other cases enter date of enlistment. Eliminate word not applicable.
2 For each enlistment give company, regiment, or arm or service with inclusive dates of service, grade, cause of discharge, number of days lost under AW 107 (if none, so state), and number of days retained and cause of retention in service for convenience of the Government, if any.
3 Enter qualifications in arms, horsemanship, etc. Show the qualification, date thereof; and number, date, and source of order announcing same.
4 See paragraph 12, AR 40-210.
5 If discharged prior to expiration of service, give number, date, and source of order or full description of authority therefor.
6 Enter periods of active duty of enlisted men of the Regular Army Reserve and the Enlisted Reserve Corps and dates of induction into Federal Service in the cases of members of the National Guard.
7 In all cases of men who are entitled to receive Certificates of Service under AR 345-500, enter here appointments and ratings held and all other items of special proficiency or merit other than those shown above.

AR 345-470.
INSTRUCTIONS FOR CERTIFICATE OF DISCHARGE
Insert name; as, "John J. Doe," in center of form.
Insert Army serial number, grade, company, regiment, or arm or service; as "1620302"; "Corporal, Company A, 1st Infantry"; "Sergeant, Quartermaster Corps."
The name and grade of the officer signing the certificate will be typewritten or printed below the signature.

U. S. GOVERNMENT PRINTING OFFICE: 1943 O - 530091

Elten, 5 November, 1946.

Dear Sir,

Today, I have an opportunity to send you the promised letter. I often think of the fine hours we were allowed to spend together beginning at our first meeting at Verona until our leave at Munich.

The hours at the Brenner, I think, were less beautiful, and I am convinced that you will always remember them, just as I do.

My journey had not the expected result, that is to be together with my family as soon as possible; but I could not manage it. 40 km away from my goal I was taken prisoner by the Russians, and I was discharged from captivity on 15 August.

I and my family are in the best of health hoping the same of you.

Hoping to hear from you soon I give you my kind regards

Yours
little fellow traveller and faithful father.

Peter Amrhein

(22a) Elten – Niederrhein
Wasserstr. 4.
Rheinprovinz
British Zone – Germany.

Lübeck, 25.4.46.

Dear Mr. Horn!

You will scarcely remember me. But I am sure you will know who I am when I tell you that on 4.4.45 I went with you from Verona to Munich.

May I ask you at first how your health is? I hope that you are well. As regards me I must say that I am not very well. But I think I shall be better in the course of time.

Now I intend to become independent. But there are certain difficulties to overcome. I rather doubt my success as during the war sufficient repairing workshops for wireless sets have been established.

It would be of great importance to me if you could confirm that I did much for you when taking you to Munich with the other officers. It is particularly important to me if you would confirm the differences I had with the SS-soldier on the Brenner, who would not allow me to go with you into the commissariat of the Red Cross, whereupon I remained in the open like you.

I leave it you to state, whether I behaved humane and correctly towards you in every respect. But I think this statement not less important to get the permit to open my independent business.

I do not understand why people who did not take part in fighting should have advantages. For an immediate answer I should be very thankful to you.

My best wishes for your future.

Yours respectfully.

Willi Lehmkuhl

Sir Horn Harvey Stanley

I write to You, so that You help me.—
I am that young lady, who from time to time came to visit You when You prisoner with other eleven your fellows by Udine in That barrack at Basaldella; do You remember this ?

Do; You yet remember the sergeant Hasselmann ? Then I did help You as I was able, also against fearfull regulations wich were there.— I am certain You remember this.— After I did come back from the Germany in Italy, I was comted to prison, and accused of collaboration wiht the german.—

I pray You, sir Lieutenant, to help me: do a declarat to my favour to the Allied Authorities, so that it is possibl I mau be free, or to renew the prosecution.—

Do this, Sir Lieutenant, and so you will Help and Comfort me and my old mother.—

Your help is only in wich I may hope.— I tank You heartly.—

I remember yet and ever I will remember You and your eleven friends, whom I pray You to salute for me.—

I remain Yours very truly

Dugar Frieda

Dugar Frieda
Via Concordia 82 - Lucinico

A veteran returns for one last flight

Editor's note: Earlier this year, Harvey Horn of Monroe told the story of his bomber group's action during World War II, including his capture and eventual release from a Nazi prison camp at the end of the war in Europe. In the following piece, Horn explains what is was like to return to his old air base in Italy nearly 60 years to the day of the navigator's last combat flight.

By Harvey Horn

I returned to the Celone Air Base in Foggia, Italy, 59 years and 332 days after my last flight as navigator on a B17 Flying Fortress, 15th Air Force, Fifth Wing, 463rd Bomb Group, 772nd Bomb Squadron.

Our mission on March 20, 1945, was to bomb the marshaling yards at Amstettin in Austria near Vienna. As they say, "A funny thing happened on the way ...."

We had to ditch our B17 - Pretty Baby Boys - into the Adriatic Sea outside of Fuime, Italy (now Rijeks, Croatia).

Unlike the weather on March 20, 1945, my wife Minerva and I left Rome on a very cold, rainy blustery day in an Avis rental car. We drove south on the A1 Autostrada to Naples, then east on A14 to Foggia.

The rain turned to snow as we approached the Apennines Mountains. The mountainside was already covered from previous snowfalls. There were stone houses in small towns dotting the hillsides.

We arrived in Foggia in mid-afternoon. The city now has a population of 155,000. The houses and government buildings were all restored.

Foggia is the birthplace of Fiorella LaGuardia, who became mayor of New York from 1933 through 1945.

Harvey Horn, second from right, is pictured above at the Amendola Air base, home to the 32nd Fight Wing of the Italian Air Force this past March. He is shown here with Luigi (Gigi) Iacomino, his wife Minerva and Lt. Marco Gismondi, commander of the 101st Fighter Squadron. The base is located northeast of Foggia, Italy, where on March 20, 1945, Horn and the rest of the crew of a B17 Flying Fortress, shown in the photo to the right, took off on a bombing run to Austria. The plane was forced to ditch in the Adriatic Sea and Horn and the crew were taken prisoners by the Germans. Horn is in the first row, second from the left.

bombed city. Today, there are still some signs of the bombings that have not been repaired.

In preparation for our visit to Foggia, I had been in contact with Luigi (Gigi) Iacomino. He has written books about Foggia during World War II and, in particular, the 463rd Bomb Group.

He also is the curator of the new museum and historian of the 32nd Fighter Wing of the Italian Air Force based in Amendola Field just northwest of Foggia.

Gigi picked us up at the Atleti Hotel for a home-cooked dinner at his house. We were greeted by 3-1/2 year old Guiseppe wearing a military cap and a waving an American flag, Gigi's mother Elena (Nona) and beautiful wife Maria-Grazia. His home was in a gated compound, protected by Max, a lovable German Shepherd. There were three other dogs but Max was the guardian of the roost.

Like most Italians, they opened up their home and hearts to us. Maria Grazia and Nona are excellent cooks. The risotto was superb. Maria Grazia gave Minerva the recipe and an Italian cookbook.

We gave the family T-shirts from New York City and West Point as well as a Teddy Bear for Guiseppe.

It is very difficult to bring presents to a family in a foreign country who you haven't met. I gave Gigi the 463rd Group Insignia, leather patches with my name and wings that was on my flight jacket for the museum. I also presented him with a copy of "My Story" about my experiences in the service.

After dinner, Gigi showed me artifacts, like a P38 Lightning Fighter Plane propeller that was designated for the Museum. He gave me a model of the first B17 Flying Fortress that he made. I was very touched.

We returned to the hotel about 10 p.m. It had been a very long day.

Promptly at 9 a.m. we were driven to the Celone Airfield. Along the way, Gigi stopped for his friend Paolo to follow us to the site. Paolo brought along a video camera to record the day.

As we drove, I tried to remember the streets of Foggia, the dirt roads, anything. But to no avail. All I could remember was being driven back to the base in the dark along with other airmen along a narrow dirt road.

After what appeared to be about five miles, we drove onto a dirt road that cut the pasture in half. I had been told that nothing remained from 1945. There was no Quonset type building that marked the end of the runway that distinguished Celone from the other airfields. All I could see this day was grass, some shrubbery.

I remembered the movie "Twelve O'clock High." It was about an adjutant who returned to the airfield of an Eighth Air Force B17 Bomber Group in England and his memories of the events that happened many years ago.

Gigi, Paolo and I got out the car. I told Minerva to remain in the car because it was very cold. The winds were blowing with such force that I wrapped my jacket hood around my face as best I could and just looked. And looked. And looked.

I couldn't believe I was really back at the air base after 60 years.

Gigi asked me what my thoughts were. I could not express them. I just stood there trying to remember 1945. I said something like how overwhelmed I was. I may have said something like I understand the feelings of others who returned to their airfields.

I walked to the side of the road and knelt down to reach for a small white rock. It is customary when you visit a Jewish cemetery to place a rock or stone on the headstone. Gigi immediately suggested that I scoop up some dirt to carry back to the states. I nodded. He found a flat piece of wood and a plastic bag and threw in three shovelfuls.

I dropped the stone in my hand and decided that the dirt would be more meaningful. This was not a grave site but a memorial of what the 463rd Bomber Group did to win the war. I also wanted to share this with my copilot, Lorin Millard.

As I started to get into the car, I looked around again at the field once more. Where had 60 years gone?

I had invited Gigi and Maria Grazia to dinner but Guiseppe was under the weather so we again were invited to dinner at their house. We told them not to prepare so much food. Gigi said "just pasta and pizza." If you believe that, I have a bridge to sell. Maria Grazia cut the number of dishes to five.

We said tearful good-byes. We will always remember Gigi and his family for taking us into their lives.

All day long, I kept thinking about why I was at a loss for words about my feelings when I looked around at the old site of the Celone field. I was sorry I didn't ask where the metal runways are, the tents, the administration building, the latrines.

Yes, I was told that all of those buildings were gone. But it didn't register until I saw for myself. It was like coming home to see the house where you grew up in was an empty lot. Even though the wind was howling, I felt a stillness, a quietness about the field.

It took 60 years to return.

I hope to return again much sooner.

Harvey Horn has been appointed commander of the Hudson Valley AM-EX POW Chapter for 2005.

The other officers are: Senior Vice Commander - Arthur Cozzavith; Junior Vice Commander - Mike Ottoman; Adjutant - Lorriane Cohen; and Treasurer - Martin Belfant.

The group's motto is: "We exist to help those who cannot help themselves."

All former POW's are invited to join. For additional information, call Horn at (845) 783-4322.

Winter 2008

GRAND CIRCLE TRAVELER

YOUR PASSPORT TO DISCOVERY AND ADVENTURE

Rijeka Revisited
On the beautiful Croatian coast, one veteran comes face-to-face with his past

On March 20, 1945, the forecast for Foggia, Italy, called for clear, sunny skies—but Harvey Horn arose long before the sun. He was preparing, along with the rest of the flight crew assigned to the B-17 "Pretty Baby's Boys," to take off at 7:00 am on a mission from Foggia's Celone Airfield.

By mid-afternoon, the sun shone brightly over Croatia's Kvarner Bay as the 772nd Bomber Squadron flew in formation toward a target just south of Vienna. One plane, however, would never reach that target. From the shore, 12-year-old Ivo Simonic and 9-year-old Stelio Vrancich watched, as "Pretty Baby's Boys" floundered over shark-infested waters—a scene that would remain impressed upon their memory, even after more than 60 years.

Ivo and Stelio weren't the only ones watching as "Pretty Baby's Boys" plummeted toward the lay at 100 miles per hour. A German Navy gunboat sat poised on the horizon, proving that sharks were not the only danger facing this struggling American crew.

"The day that changed my world"

Thinking back to that fateful day, Harvey could not possibly have imagined that 62 years later, he'd be planning a return to Croatia—this time on a very different mission.

In 1945, the flak-damaged "Pretty Baby's Boys" had flown low over a coastal town before finally hitting the waters of Kvarner Bay. Back then, the town was known as Fiume, Italy—but after the war it was returned to Croatia (then part of Yugoslavia) and renamed "Rijeka." It was a changed town to which Harvey would be returning, having

Harvey Horn (left) talks with reporter Denis Romac during his return visit to Rijeka, Croatia.

grown from a population of 55,000 in 1945 to more than 255,000 in 2007—the third-largest city in a now-independent Croatia. Harvey, too, was much changed—indeed, since March 20, 1945, he has never been the same.

After losing power in all but one of the plane's four engines, Harvey and his nine crewmates were forced to ditch "Pretty Baby's Boys" in Kvarner Bay—that they all survived is a

CONTINUED FROM PAGE 1

remarkable feat and a testament to the great skill of the plane's pilot and copilot. As the crew began to paddle toward safety, the German Navy approached them. "I can still see the soldiers pointing their rifles at us as we neared our rubber boats," Harvey remembers. After spending one night imprisoned in Fiume, unsure as to whether their lives would be spared, the ten were transferred to an SS prison in Trieste, Italy, for interrogation. Five days later, they began the arduous journey to Stalag 13D, a POW camp in Nurnberg, Germany, where they would spend the remainder of the war.

"It took many years for me to recognize the latent emotional effects of being shot down, surviving a ditching into the sea, and being Jewish and captured by the Germans," Harvey recalls. He returned to Rijeka, he says, "to complete a circle."

A plan to return

Harvey, along with his wife, Minerva, chose *Dubrovnik & Beyond: From the Adriatic to the Alps* as their sixth Grand Circle vacation. Knowing that the Escorted Tour featured a visit to Rijeka, Harvey embraced the opportunity to revisit his past. "I wanted to learn if there were any documents or newspaper articles recording the event," Harvey says, "which must have been witnessed by the people of Fiume/Rijeka." He began his search at the Croatian Consulate in New York City—which led him to Wanda Radetti, Commercial and Cultural Attaché to the City of Rijeka and *Condé Nast Traveler's* top destination specialist for Croatia. She used her considerable contacts to arrange for Harvey and Minerva to meet Mayor Vojko Obersnel in Rijeka on February 23, 2007.

As he approached Rijeka for the first time

A hero's welcome

On February 23, a private car picked up Harvey and Minerva from their hotel in nearby Opatija and drove them to Rijeka's City Hall. Harvey presented Mayor Obersnel with a letter of friendship from Mayor John Karl, Jr., of his hometown of Monroe, New York. He also gave him a framed "Certificate of Appreciation" from the Hudson Valley Chapter of the Prisoners of War, in recognition of the Croatian partisans who had helped downed American flyers during World War II. Among these partisans, Harvey learned, were Mayor Obersnel's parents.

In turn, Mayor Obersnel presented Harvey with a book called *Rijeka Revisited*, a cultural and historic account of the city. Minerva received a beautiful bouquet of flowers and a cravat. Then, the Horns met with Denis Romac, a reporter from the largest newspaper in the region, who interviewed Harvey for more than an hour—a meeting that would prove to have powerful consequences.

After joining Wanda Radetti for a sumptuous lunch at Rijeka's Hotel Bonavia, Harvey had something important to tend to. "With Denis, we walked to the waterfront, which was rebuilt some years ago," Harvey says. "I took petals from Minerva's bouquet and threw them into the sea. It's a ceremony that our POW chapter conducts to remember all POWs who have served our country since revolutionary days."

"One day at a time …"

Harvey had first contacted the Croatian

ABOVE: Today, the city of Rijeka on Kvarner Bay is Croatia's largest seaport. AT RIGHT: To Harvey Horn during World War II, Rijeka—then Fiume, Italy—looked very, very different.

Twelve-year-old Ivo Simonic was sitting with a friend on a slope above Fiume when they heard the roar of the damaged bomber. The boys ran to see where the plane was flying, and encountered two German SS officers. Ivo remembers hearing one of them say, "Those must be damned good pilots, able to ditch such a plane perfectly." He also remembers that it happened on a beautiful sunny day.

While not a witness to the crash, another man contacted Harvey after reading his story. Danijel Frka, a photographer, deep sea diver, and author of a book called *Secrets of the Adriatic Sea*, has made four dives so far in an effort to locate the wreckage of "Pretty Baby's Boys." When he succeeds in retrieving the sunken bomber, Harvey plans to return to Rijeka once more, this time in the company of his fellow survivors.

Until then, Harvey can complete the circle begun on March 20, 1945, with fond memories of his return to Rijeka—and while he had trouble articulating his feelings immediately

Nurnberg, Germany, where they would spend the remainder of the war.

"It took many years for me to recognize the latent emotional effects of being shot down, surviving a ditching into the sea, and being Jewish and captured by the Germans," Harvey recalls. He returned to Rijeka, he says, "to complete a circle."

A plan to return

Harvey, along with his wife, Minerva, chose *Dubrovnik & Beyond: From the Adriatic to the Alps* as their sixth Grand Circle vacation. Knowing that the Escorted Tour featured a visit to Rijeka, Harvey embraced the opportunity to revisit his past. "I wanted to learn if there were any documents or newspaper articles recording the event," Harvey says, "which must have been witnessed by the people of Fiume/Rijeka." He began his search at the Croatian Consulate in New York City—which led him to Wanda Radetti, Commercial and Cultural Attaché to the City of Rijeka and *Condé Nast Traveler's* top destination specialist for Croatia. She used her considerable contacts to arrange for Harvey and Minerva to meet Mayor Vojko Obersnel in Rijeka on February 23, 2007.

As he approached Rijeka for the first time since 1945, Harvey was awash in memories. "Last time, I was high above Rijeka (then Fiume), bracing for the inevitable jolt of our plane hitting the water at 100 miles per hour," he recalls. This time, he surveyed Kvarner Bay from the safety of a Grand Circle motorcoach—and he was about to enjoy an infinitely warmer reception.

Harvey Horn during World War II, Rijeka—then Fiume, Italy—looked very, very different.

from the Hudson Valley Chapter of the Prisoners of War, in recognition of the Croatian partisans who had helped downed American flyers during World War II. Among these partisans, Harvey learned, were Mayor Obersnel's parents.

In turn, Mayor Obersnel presented Harvey with a book called *Rijeka Revisited*, a cultural and historic account of the city. Minerva received a beautiful bouquet of flowers and a cravat. Then, the Horns met with Denis Romac, a reporter from the largest newspaper in the region, who interviewed Harvey for more than an hour—a meeting that would prove to have powerful consequences.

After joining Wanda Radetti for a sumptuous lunch at Rijeka's Hotel Bonavia, Harvey had something important to tend to. "With Denis, we walked to the waterfront, which was rebuilt some years ago," Harvey says. "I took petals from Minerva's bouquet and threw them into the sea. It's a ceremony that our POW chapter conducts to remember all POWs who have served our country since revolutionary days."

"One day at a time …"

Harvey had first contacted the Croatian consulate in hopes that he might find locals who witnessed his crash—and after the story appeared in Croatian newspapers, he finally got his wish. Though Stelio Vrancich, a cousin of Wanda Radetti, was only nine years old when he watched smoke stream from the engine of "Pretty Baby's Boys," he still remembers the plane's descent over Fiume.

Twelve-year-old Ivo Simonic was sitting with a friend on a slope above Fiume when they heard the roar of the damaged bomber. The boys ran to see where the plane was flying, and encountered two German SS officers. Ivo remembers hearing one of them say, "Those must be damned good pilots, able to ditch such a plane perfectly." He also remembers that it happened on a beautiful sunny day.

While not a witness to the crash, another man contacted Harvey after reading his story. Danijel Frka, a photographer, deep sea diver, and author of a book called *Secrets of the Adriatic Sea*, has made four dives so far in an effort to locate the wreckage of "Pretty Baby's Boys." When he succeeds in retrieving the sunken bomber, Harvey plans to return to Rijeka once more, this time in the company of his fellow survivors.

Until then, Harvey can complete the circle begun on March 20, 1945, with fond memories of his return to Rijeka—and while he had trouble articulating his feelings immediately following his visit, he has since come to an enlightening conclusion: "Each day, events occur that we cannot explain or are beyond our control," Harvey says. "I learned that you have to enjoy each day, one day at a time."

www.ingramcontent.com/pod-product-compliance
Lightning Source LLC
Chambersburg PA
CBHW081459040426
42446CB00016B/3315